CW00969281

A VERY ENGLISH HANGMAN

Albert Pierrepoint

A VERY ENGLISH HANGMAN

The Life and Times of Albert Pierrepoint

LEONORA KLEIN

CORVO

First published in Great Britain in 2006 by
Corvo Books Ltd
64 Duncan Terrace
London, N1 8AG
www.corvobooks.com

A catalogue record for this book is available from the British Library.

Jacket design by Richard Roberts
Author photograph by Tom Garside
Typeset by SJM Design
Image on page 241 © Getty Images
All other images © Michael and Doreen Forman

Printed and bound in Great Britain by
The Cromwell Press, Wiltshire.

ISBN: 0-9543255-6-7

CONTENTS

ACKNOWLEDGEMENTS

I would like to thank everyone who has given me their time and their thoughts on Pierrepoint, including Robert Harris, Daniel Janner, Andrew Mitchell, Fred Wright, Cyril Moss, Tony Wolstenholme and Michael and Doreen Forman. In particular I would like to thank Tommy Mann, who was so generous with his time and so kind and courteous in putting up with my endless questions.

I am very grateful to the staff at the British Library, the National Archives, the Mass Observation Archive, the Imperial War Museum and the Wolfson Crime, Punishment and Law Archive. Thanks also go to Susanna Lamb at Madame Tussauds and Martina Skrabakova at the Cambridge Union, Roy Ingleton, Carol Bennion, Roy Winton, to all the members of NARPO who kindly took the time to respond to my questions, and to Eric Dobby for allowing me to use text from Albert Pierrepoint's autobiography.

Special thanks to Richard Holmes and Kathryn Hughes, who made me think that it would be possible to write a book, and to my editor, Julia Rochester, who made it happen. Thank you to Rudolf Klein for being a great critic and, most importantly, to Peter Moffat, who has lived with Pierrepoint for too long.

INTRODUCTION

I never intended to write a book about Albert Pierrepoint. I came across his autobiography by chance when I was researching a minor suffragette. It was next to the books on Holloway prison and the spine caught my attention: 'Executioner: Pierrepoint', red on black, very lurid. I picked it up; just a quick break, I thought, from all those earnest bonnets. This was the dedication at the front of the book: 'To ANNE, my wife who in forty years never asked a question I dedicate this book with grateful thanks for her loyalty and discretion.'

Three months later I am sitting in the tea rooms of the Adelphi Hotel in Liverpool, waiting for the Mayor of Sefton. The tea rooms might once have been a ballroom, and they had certainly seen happier days; now the guests are scattered amongst acres of pink carpet, stranded in their armchairs, hoping for biscuits. Tommy Mann is tall, with a reassuringly confident manner and a kind face. He insists on buying my tea and later, when we leave, he holds the door open for me. He has come to talk to me about his old friend, Albert Pierrepoint. He knew him for more than thirty years and when Pierrepoint died, in 1992, Tommy gave the eulogy at his funeral. That afternoon, in the Adelphi, he tells me an extraordinary story.

In his retirement, living quietly with his wife in a bungalow in

Southport, Pierrepoint kept a suitcase under the bed. One day, when Tommy Mann was visiting his old friend, Pierrepoint took him into the bedroom and showed him the contents of the suitcase. Inside were his execution diaries, letters, photographs, a piece of rope, a white hood and something that looked like a small leather belt. The diaries contained a list of names, dates, and technical details. The letters were from friends and public figures, expressing respect and admiration. The photographs showed the bodies of the Nazi war criminals who Pierrepoint hanged in 1945. The leather belt was the strap that Pierrepoint used to tie the hands of the condemned prisoner before he was taken to the scaffold. The white hood covered his head before the rope was placed around his neck. Pierrepoint put the hood over Tommy's head and tied his hands behind his back with the strap. Then he said with a laugh, 'You're the only man who has walked away from Albert Pierrepoint.'

Tommy told me that the strap was made of thick, soft leather and one of the eyelets was ripped. Paraphernalia and memorabilia – kept out of sight, inside a suitcase, under the bed he shared with the wife who never asked any questions, who was loyal and discreet.

I was fascinated and at the same time I felt deeply uneasy about my fascination; I have always believed, and will always believe, that capital punishment is morally and ethically indefensible, so why did I want to write about an executioner? During the French Revolution, when Marie Tussaud was working as a young apprentice, she was sent to the cemetery in Paris to collect the newly guillotined heads of aristocrats so that her master could model their death masks in wax before they began to disintegrate. Now the Chamber of Horrors at Madame Tussauds has remodelled its own history, and a gruesome wax tableau shows the figure of Marie picking her way through gravestones and piles of headless bodies, searching for notable heads. Next to this tableau the wax heads of Robespierre, Marie Antoinette and Louis XVI are displayed in a glass case, modelled from the original death masks. And next to them is the guillotine: the original blade, the one that beheaded Marie Antoinette. I was afraid that if I pursued the story of the suitcase, I would become another Marie Tussaud, with blood on my hands, but I wanted to know more about this man.

Pierrepoint's career as an executioner began in 1932 and ended in 1956. For nearly a quarter of a century he was called upon by the state to go inside the walls of the prison and hang people. As I followed Pierrepoint's story I realised that if I was going to understand him, I needed to investigate his relationship to the state and to the system that made him. Pierrepoint performed his duties in private. When he was inside the prison walls he was in charge, he was the boss. Outside the prison walls it was different; the job never changed, but during Pierrepoint's time its significance changed radically. After the Second World War he was the public face of British justice, paid to hang Nazi war criminals quickly and efficiently, paid to hang John Amery, who had betrayed his country. In the 1950s he executed Timothy Evans, Derek Bentley and Ruth Ellis and he became implicated in the controversy that surrounded those cases. Pierrepoint was famous for his speed and his discretion; he perfected the role of official executioner and made it his own, just as it went out of fashion. He resigned in 1956, at the moment when the abolition of capital punishment was becoming a political reality and the chief executioner was becoming a political liability.

The judicial and political system that condemned people to

death – whether they were Nazi war criminals or night-club hostesses – depended, finally, upon Pierrepoint. The police who made the arrest, the barristers who appeared at the trial, the judges who handed down the sentence of death and the Home Secretaries to whom they appealed for mercy all played a part in a process that ended on the scaffold, with Pierrepoint. Some of them admired what he did, others were disgusted by it. The police wanted a hangman and they admired Pierrepoint; the government needed a hangman but they were disgusted by the reality of what they were asking him to do on their behalf. They are all a part of Pierrepoint's story.

The last public execution in England took place in 1868. Hanging, in its public manifestation, had become shameful and therefore something that had to be hidden. In order to survive, hanging had to be useful to the state; it still had to create a useful terror, but it had to be represented in a different way. The state had to maintain a delicate balance between concealment and disclosure. Concealment of shame, disclosure of justice. The hangman was entrusted with the act, and the concealment depended upon his co-operation and his discretion. The suitcase was hidden, but Pierrepoint had the key. He performed the act in private and undertook the concealment in public. The hangman stood at the centre; he was both an actor and a cipher in the conflict between concealment and disclosure. It was a delicate balancing act, a particularly English balancing act between the public and the private. Pierrepoint was England's hangman.

CHAPTER ONE

A Brief Life

Pierrepoint's autobiography was published in 1974, when the world he was describing had disappeared. With the help of his ghostwriter Pierrepoint gives an account of his childhood which belongs to a particular tradition of working-class family history, one that celebrates respectability, shared values and solidarity. A sentimental portrait of a deferential community.

Pierrepoint was born in 1905 in Clayton, Yorkshire, the eldest son in a family of five children. His father, Henry, was one of ten children, and he began work in the mills at the age of twelve. Later Henry worked as a carrier and a butcher's apprentice, but the jobs never lasted. When Pierrepoint was five years old the family abandoned village life in Clayton and moved to Huddersfield. Henry worked in the gasworks and the ironworks but there were periods of unemployment when the Pierrepoint children had to rely on the local Mission for free clogs. According to his son, Henry Pierrepoint was a warm, loving and occasionally unreliable father. He liked a drink. His mother was a model of wifely tolerance and maternal virtue, long-suffering, hard working and loyal. Christmas meant an orange and a few nuts, but the poverty was respectable. Pierrepoint glosses over the hardships of his childhood and he describes his father as a popular, feckless charmer. In fact there were times when the family was in dire straits; Pierrepoint may not have known, or may have chosen not to mention, that on at least one occasion his father was driven to write a desperate begging letter.

Perhaps it is his father's desperation that lies behind the cheery platitudes of the childhood that Pierrepoint describes in his autobiography.

Pierrepoint was nine years old when the First World War started and he describes being taken to a show at the Bradford Palace Theatre, where there was a lot of patriotic singing and waving of Union Jacks before George Formby came on. The war helped at home because his mother got a job in a munitions factory, filling artillery shells. Then, in the summer of 1916, things changed in the Pierrepoint household; Uncle Johnny, Pierrepoint's maternal uncle, was killed in the Battle of the Somme and his father became involved in some mysterious business, something that was not explained to young Pierrepoint.

One evening that summer Pierrepoint was standing outside a pub in the centre of Bradford, waiting for his father. He noticed a poster outside a newspaper shop. He recognised the man in the photograph. It was his father. Then he read the headline underneath the photograph: 'MY TEN YEARS' EXPERIENCE, BY HENRY A. PIERREPOINT RETIRED EXECUTIONER.' At that moment Henry came out of the pub with a friend and introduced him to his son,

> 'This is my eldest son,' he said. 'And one day *he* will be the Official Executioner.' I looked up at my father and my mind was suddenly very clear. My mission, my

> one-man expedition, I knew what it was. And I knew what it needed. 'Our Dad,' I said, 'Can I go into long trousers?' He looked at me with all the pride in the world. 'Yes, our Albert,' he said. 'You can. I'll speak to your mother about it.'

This is Pierrepoint's rite of passage, the moment when his past and future are revealed to him and he receives his father's blessing. It is a moment of revelation because up to this point the young boy has not understood the reason for his father's 'mysterious apartness'. The revelation is extended to his much adored Uncle Tom, his father's older brother; he too is an executioner. Whether or not Pierrepoint really spent the first eleven years of his life in ignorance of the fact that his father and his uncle were executioners, he chose to describe it this way in his autobiography. He eventually confesses to the more secular attractions of his calling – social status and foreign travel – but throughout his book he returns to the idea of a revelation that gave rise to a mission or a calling.

Henry Pierrepoint's reminiscences were serialised every Saturday in *Thomson's Weekly News*, starting in July 1916 and running until the end of the year. The first instalment appeared on the front page of the paper and, alongside a photograph of Henry, dark and handsome with a well-kept moustache, there was an introduction: 'The word "hangman" almost invariably evokes a shiver from over-sensitive persons. They imagine him a morose, blood-thirsty sort of villain … Well, I have a charming wife and a family of young children, and I would refer you to them as to whether I am anything in the way of a brutal villain.' Each week for five months every member of the family read the stories, on their own, in private. No one spoke about them because Mary Pierrepoint did not permit any conversation about her husband's job. Pierrepoint read and reread the stories and he was thrilled by them. Henry was a natural storyteller and his job had taken him all over the country; Pierrepoint had never travelled more than thirty miles from home and his father's account of a trip to Jersey seemed to him an exotic adventure on the high seas. Henry's stories were the myths and legends of Pierrepoint's childhood, to be studied in secret, a clandestine pleasure. They were also a substitute for the real thing: Pierrepoint was five years old when Henry carried out his last execution. Henry was the first executioner in the family, but he only did the job for ten years. He was never officially sacked, but in 1910 the work just dried up.

In his autobiography Pierrepoint implies that Henry's early retirement may have had something to do with the difficulties that existed between Henry and a man called John Ellis, who succeeded Henry as executioner. He suggests that there may have been foul play, inspired by professional jealousy, and he is very anxious that his readers should be clear about one thing: his father's retirement was not in any way connected with any kind of professional misconduct.

What Pierrepoint does not tell his readers is that when Henry arrived at Chelmsford prison on 13 July 1910 to prepare for an execution the following day, he was drunk. For no apparent reason, Henry started shouting abuse at his assistant and physically assaulted him. He was restrained but he continued to shout abuse. The Governor of the prison arranged for the two men to eat their meals separately and sleep in different rooms. The execution took place the next morning as planned. The incident was witnessed by the Governor and two prison officers, all of whom made statements to the Prison Commission.

Afterwards the assistant wrote to the Commission, expressing surprise at Pierrepoint's animosity and requesting that the Commissioners take action: 'Up to yesterday, we have never had a cross word, I have always given him the best advice possible, to take drink in moderation, and always to turn up at the Prison sober, as when the public saw him drunk, it always caused a lot of unnecessary talk, and it gave them the impression, that he had to get drunk to do his work, and that they had a bad opinion of us all that are on the Home Office list, and we were the lowest of the low.' The assistant was John Ellis. On 22 July 1910 Henry's name was removed from the list of executioners and he never worked again as an official executioner.

On 1 May 1911 Henry wrote to the Home Secretary. In this letter he admits that he had 'a few words' with Ellis on 13 July 1910, but he explains that he was only defending himself from Ellis's repeated attempts to do him out of work: 'I could have reported him many times had I taken the trouble. But I never did a man out of his work under handed nor never will ... I have a wife and five young children to keep and I can assure you that I have had a lot to bear. I should be pleased if you would only communicate with the Rev. Benjamin Gregory of the Huddersfield Mission.' Five years later *Thomson's Weekly News* paid Henry for his hangman's stories. Executioners were not supposed to drink on duty and they were not supposed to publish their memoirs, but they had been doing both for years.

In 1884 the public executioner was a man called Bartholomew Binns, who turned up drunk to executions and was in the habit of visiting the local pubs afterwards to show off his ropes. His behaviour became so intemperate that, holding its nose and stepping delicately to avoid the mire, *The Times* was reluctantly drawn into the debate: 'The common hangman is an unsavoury and repulsive subject, which we should be very glad to leave severely alone. But it is, unfortunately, impossible to ignore the scandals which occur with almost unfailing regularity every time the present public executioner has to do his ghastly office.'

By 1913 Pierrepoint's Uncle Tom was number two to John Ellis, who had succeeded Henry as chief executioner. Ellis was a barber from Rochdale who bred bulldogs and executed somewhere in the region of 200 people in the first quarter of the twentieth century. His business notepaper announced him as 'John Ellis, Umbrella Repairer, Stationer, Hairdresser etc.' Ellis resigned in 1923, leaving Uncle Tom as the number one executioner, and returned to his barber's business and his dog breeding. Five months after his resignation, Ellis tried to kill himself. He shot himself in the jaw but survived and was prosecuted for attempted suicide. The Chairman of the Rochdale Bench elicited an undertaking from Ellis that he would not make another attempt: 'I am very sorry to see you here, Ellis. If your aim had been as straight as the drops you have given it would have been a bad job for you. Your life has been lengthened and I hope you will make the best use of it … My colleagues want me to say that in your own interests as well as the interests of your wife it would be advisable for you to give up the drink.' Ellis returned unhappily to the shop and the dogs and supplemented his income by selling his story.

In 1924 *Thomson's Weekly News* serialised Ellis's reminiscences and although the newspaper promised that he would 'relate many hitherto unrevealed things', the Home Office did nothing to stop him. The minutes on the Home Office files make it very clear what the problem was: 'There are many objections to such publications and some people no doubt criticise the authorities for not preventing publication. But if there were clear means of prevention, and use were made of them, it might then be alleged that the authorities were afraid to have people know how executions are carried out.'

Ellis hit the headlines again three years later when he appeared in a play about the murderer Charlie Peace. His first entrance at the Grand in Gravesend came in the closing moments of the play, when he appeared in a black suit with a white silk handkerchief in his breast pocket and hanged Charlie Peace. The headlines were high-pitched: 'Hangman-cum-Showman: Storm of Protest. Should Ellis enact the gallows scene?' squealed the *Daily Herald*. Questions were asked in the House of Commons and a week later the play closed.

In 1932 Ellis once again resorted to public entertainment as a way to make a living and he began touring country fairs, giving demonstrations in hanging. Once again questions were asked in the House of Commons and once again the Home Office felt powerless to stop Ellis. The minutes on the file reveal an issue that was never resolved: 'The only means by which control could be established over the actions of former executioners would be to create a public and pensionable office of executioner, as part of the prison service. There are obvious objections to this especially from the point of view of unfavourable reactions on the mentality of the service.'

This goes to the heart of the tension between the government and the hangman. The Home Office was suffering from an attack of political queasiness: so long as capital punishment was on the statute book, the government needed a hangman, but no politician wanted to be seen shaking his hand, let alone giving him a pension. The ex-hangman continued to look elsewhere for his income.

By the end of the summer of 1932 Ellis had tired of his fairground shows. He was suffering from poor health and depression and he returned to the barber's shop in Rochdale. On

22 September 1932 the *Daily Mail* carried a piece from their Special Correspondent in Rochdale: 'A fawn-coloured whippet, slow of foot and toothless, is today mourning its master – John Ellis, for twenty-three years the public hangman, who yesterday cut his throat after chasing his wife and daughter from the house in terror.'

Uncle Tom, who never sold his story to the newspapers, became the chief executioner and he was Pierrepoint's role model. Pierrepoint always portrayed him as a sober and dignified man, who had learnt from his brother's example and from his mistakes. Thomas Pierrepoint's career as an executioner spanned most of the first half of the twentieth century and although he did not have a colourful public persona like his brother Henry, documents that have just been released in the National Archives suggest that he, too, may have struggled with drink. He was not quite the paragon of virtue that his nephew described.

In 1917 Henry Pierrepoint and his family left Huddersfield and moved to Failsworth, near Manchester. The furniture was piled into a large wagon and pulled across the Yorkshire moors by two horses, with Pierrepoint and his younger brother sitting on top of the tables and chairs. Their new home was in Mill Street and Pierrepoint went to the local school – Holy Trinity. Later he attended the Unitarian church, motivated by his love of football, rather than a spiritual conversion; the Unitarians were better footballers than the Catholics and attendance at Sunday school was a prerequisite for joining the team, so Pierrepoint became a regular. He left school at thirteen, just before the end of the First World War, and worked in the spinning mills. It was hard, thankless work but Pierrepoint says that he wanted to earn, to help his mother. Later he felt that he had missed out, and regretted his lack of formal education, but at the time money seemed more important.

It was not only Henry's feckless nature that inspired Pierrepoint's sense of filial duty; his father was ill and gradually he became incapable of doing any physical work. In 1922 Henry started writing, and he filled two blue exercise books with the story of his life as a hangman. Once again his story was published, this time by *Reynolds News*, and in December of the same year Henry died. He left Pierrepoint three books: the blue exercise books and one other, a black book. The black book was Henry Pierrepoint's execution diary, a record of every hanging that he had carried out. It was his legacy. Pierrepoint was seventeen years old when Henry died: 'The death of my father marked the end of my boyhood.'

In 1960 Ted Willis, who created *Dixon of Dock Green*, published a fictional autobiography, *Dixon of Dock Green: My Life by George Dixon*. It is an affectionate chronicle of a working-class boyhood in Dock Green, where work is scarce and life is hard, but hearts are made of gold. Dad is on the dole but mum always makes ends meet. Dad is struggling with unemployment but young George has his role model in Uncle Bert, a country policeman. In exactly this style, Pierrepoint's autobiography describes his summer holidays with Uncle Tom and Aunt Lizzie in Clayton, relishing the ginger beer and spice cake, and in a similar fantasy of escape the fictional George spends his holidays in a thatched cottage in Essex, home of Uncle Bert and Aunt Emily. Like Pierrepoint's Uncle Tom, who worked as a carrier when he wasn't hanging people, Uncle Bert the bobby is a respected local figure and an inspiration for the young boy. George leaves school at fourteen, a year later than Pierrepoint, and, like Pierrepoint, works in a series of jobs before he starts the job that will become his life's work. When George's dad dies, it is Bert who saves the day by suggesting that George should become a policeman. This is George's long-trousers moment: 'Suddenly I wanted to be a policeman, more than anything I could ever remember wanting before.'

When his father died Pierrepoint became the head of the household, the man on whom his mother could rely, and he remained at home for twenty years, always a dutiful son. Dutiful, but not dull. He had inherited his father's charm and he liked to sing and go to dances. Ruth Johnson was a local girl who remembered Pierrepoint: 'He was a quiet and attractive young man, quite a favourite at the Saturday night dances.' Pierrepoint worked hard, battling like everyone else through the depression of the 1920s. Eventually he left the mills and started to work as a horse drayman for a wholesale grocer's company, delivering to the local shops. By 1930 horses were no longer being used and Pierrepoint had the satisfaction of being one of the first men in the district to drive a lorry. This was something, but it wasn't enough; he still nurtured his secret ambition, fed by his father's stories. Tom had never spoken to his nephew about his job, but Pierrepoint knew, and he read the newspaper reports of executions, envying his uncle, following his progress. In 1931, when he was twenty-six years old, Pierrepoint wrote to the Prison Commissioners, offering his services as an assistant executioner. To his dismay, they turned him down – the lists were full. He had told no one about his application and he nursed his disappointment in private.

Six months later Pierrepoint received another letter from the Prison Commissioners. A vacancy had come up and he was invited to Strangeways prison in Manchester for an interview. His mother recognised the official envelope. It was thirty years since her husband had first assisted at an execution, and finally she broke her silence: 'You're after your father's job, aren't you?' Mary Pierrepoint had always hated her husband's job, and she didn't want her son to follow in his father's footsteps. Pierrepoint says that his mother found the job repugnant, but this didn't seem to trouble him greatly: 'She recognised my resolve, and having done so, never made another protest.' According to Pierrepoint, they never spoke about it again. The whole episode is framed as a tribute to his mother's delicate sensibility and quiet fortitude. Her repugnance becomes a natural expression of her femininity, rather than a serious objection worthy of his consideration.

Pierrepoint got through the interview at Strangeways; the next hurdle was four days of training and assessment at Pentonville prison in London. The midnight train from Manchester came into Euston at six o'clock in the morning. Pierrepoint walked for three hours: Trafalgar Square, Whitehall, the Cenotaph, the Home Office, Scotland Yard. It was another world. Outside the Home Office there was a brass plate to identify the building – he reached out and touched it, for luck. Then he took the number 77 bus to Pentonville prison. There he had another interview, a medical examination and four days of instruction in the execution chamber. He learnt how to calculate the drop, how to adjust the ropes, how to fix the noose. Using a dummy, he was taken through his paces: placing the white cap over the head, putting the noose around the neck, releasing the safety pin on the lever that opened the trapdoors, pushing the lever down, releasing the trapdoors. Quickly, smoothly, without a moment's hesitation, a tutorial in efficient killing: 'Cap, noose, pin, push, drop.' Again and again and again. At the end of the four days the Governor gave him an oral examination and watched him execute the dummy. He took the train back to Manchester and waited. The letter came at the end of September 1932: he was in. Pierrepoint's name had been added to the list of people who were competent to act as assistant executioners.

Enclosed with the letter was a 'Memorandum of Conditions to which any Person acting as Assistant Executioner is required to conform.' This memorandum included the following rules:

> Rule 6: He should avoid attracting public attention in going to or from the prison; he should clearly understand that his conduct and general behaviour must be respectable and discreet, not only at the place and time of execution, but before and subsequently; in particular he must not give to any person particulars on the subject of his duty for publication.
>
> Rule 9: The name of any person who does not give satisfaction or whose conduct is in any way objectionable so as to cast discredit on himself, either in connection with the duties or otherwise, will be removed from the list.

The pay was £1.11.6d for each execution, followed by another £1.11.6d, 'if his conduct and behaviour are satisfactory, during and subsequent to the execution'. Pierrepoint was earning £2.5s a week delivering groceries, so the extra income was not a huge amount, particularly since the executioner and his assistant had to report to the prison by four o'clock in the afternoon on the day before the execution, which meant that each execution would mean the loss of two days' wages. The fees for a chief executioner were better; in 1951, when average weekly earnings for men over twenty-one were £8, Pierrepoint carried out fifteen executions and he was paid an average of £10 for each one, plus expenses. The money was important to Pierrepoint, but it was not his reason for doing the job.

On Christmas Day 1932 Pierrepoint, his mother and his sister, Ivy, gathered around the wireless to hear George V give the first Christmas Message, broadcast live from Sandringham: 'Through one of the marvels of modern science, I am enabled this Christmas Day to speak to all my peoples throughout the Empire.' Two days later Pierrepoint stood on the freezing dockside at Holyhead; Uncle Tom had been engaged for an execution in Mountjoy prison, Dublin, and Pierrepoint was to be his assistant. At last, ten years after the death of his father, he had embarked on his first adventure and, according to Pierrepoint's autobiography, the first chapter was a real swashbuckler. Before they had even set off, Pierrepoint discovered that Tom was carrying a large revolver. British executioners were not popular in the Irish Free State and although Tom kept the gun and the bullets in different pockets, it gave him a sense of security. Mostly, though, they would be protected by their own reticence and discretion: Tom had executed a lot of men in Dublin, but although his name was known, his face was not. Tom was very clear: from the moment they set out, there would be no conversation between them about the reason for their journey.

The two men spent most of the night crossing in the ship's bar, where a group of Guinness-drinking Catholic priests persuaded Pierrepoint to entertain them with his repertoire of Irish songs. Pierrepoint rose to the occasion and they were entranced. Uncle Tom was proud of his charming, musical nephew, and Pierrepoint, brimful with the excitement of their secret mission and flattered by an appreciative audience, felt that his new life had truly begun. This, almost more than the execution itself, was his debut. His public performance was inspired by a sense of his new responsibilities, his great task, made greater still by the secrecy that surrounded it. In his autobiography Pierrepoint is at pains to say that it was not the drink that moved him: Uncle Tom sipped his ale, and Pierrepoint drank Bovril. He was following in his father's footsteps, but his journey would be different.

Just before eight o'clock the next morning Pierrepoint and his uncle stood outside the condemned cell in Mountjoy prison, waiting for the signal to enter. Tom was very calm and he was sucking a sweet, which was his habit before an execution. At eight o'clock they entered the cell and less than a minute later Patrick McDermott was dead. Pierrepoint had done exactly what was required of him: he had followed his uncle onto the scaffold, strapped McDermott's legs together and then moved quickly away, before the trapdoors opened. Pierrepoint was impressed by the speed of the execution, but otherwise he was unmoved. Afterwards, he followed his uncle's example and refused the glass of whiskey that was offered to him. They left the prison and passed, unnoticed, through the angry crowds who were waiting for the executioner to emerge.

Throughout the 1930s Pierrepoint looked after his mother and carried on with his work in the grocery business. He also assisted at thirty-two executions, almost always working alongside his uncle, learning the trade. Pierrepoint was a keen pupil and Tom had thirty years of experience. Together, they travelled across England: to London, Exeter, Gloucester, Durham and Liverpool. They were a team, a family firm, popular with prison officers, affectionately known as 'Our Albert' and 'Uncle Tom', but also respected and admired. Pierrepoint believed that Tom brought dignity to the office of chief executioner, and that was what really impressed him: dignity and discretion. The men (and women) they executed were rarely monstrous psychopaths; mostly they were ordinary people who had done a terrible thing, driven by jealousy, or lust, or greed – husbands, lovers, burglars, people who could have had different lives.

'Uncle Tom' and 'Our Albert'

On 10 May 1940 Chamberlain's Conservative government gave way to a National Coalition led by Winston Churchill. By the middle of June the French Government had capitulated and northern France was subjected to German military occupation. Pierrepoint's sister, Ivy, was a volunteer nurse and when the British Expeditionary Force was evacuated from Dunkirk she worked eighteen-hour shifts in the operating theatre. She died shortly afterwards and Pierrepoint always believed that she had died of exhaustion. After Dunkirk Britain began to prepare for what seemed inevitable: a German invasion. The whole of the south coast of England became a 'Defence Area' and civilian movement was severely restricted. Two government leaflets – 'Stay Where You Are' and 'If the Invader Comes' – were distributed to every household.

In the summer of 1940 the Germans launched an air offensive against Britain as a prelude to the invasion. The figures for the Battle of Britain are still shocking: between July and October 1940 the *Luftwaffe* lost more than 1,700 aeroplanes and the RAF lost more than 900. In July London had not yet become a target, but it was preparing for the worst. Churchill was rallying the nation and Pierrepoint, still in Yorkshire, where his food deliveries had been deemed an essential wartime service, was listening: 'We await undismayed the impending assault ... We shall defend every village, town and city. The vast mass of London itself, fought street by street, could easily devour an entire hostile army, and we would rather see London laid in ruins and ashes than that it should be tamely and abjectly enslaved.'

A few weeks later Pierrepoint came to London to assist at the execution of Udham Singh. As a teenager in the Punjab, Singh had witnessed the 1919 Amritsar massacre, which took place in the midst of violent protests against the oppressive Rowlatt Acts. There were riots in the Punjabi city of Amritsar, sacred capital of the Sikhs, and several English residents were killed. Three days later General Dyer ordered British troops to open fire without warning on a peaceful protest meeting of some 10,000 unarmed men, women and children. Three hundred and seventy-nine people were killed and more than 1200 were wounded. Twenty-one years later, on 13 March 1940 in Caxton Hall in

London, at a meeting of the East India Association, Udham Singh took his revenge: he shot and killed one of the speakers at the meeting, Sir Michael O'Dwyer, who had been Governor of the Punjab at the time of the massacre: 'He was the real culprit. He deserved it. He wanted to crush the spirit of my people, so I [had to] crush him.'

Four months after he shot O'Dwyer, as London prepared for a German attack, Singh was executed at Pentonville. Pierrepoint was the assistant and a man called Stanley Cross carried out the execution. It was his first time as chief executioner and, according to Pierrepoint, he wasn't up to the job. The evening before the execution, Cross had to calculate the drop and prepare the gallows. Observed by the Governor and the Sheriff, Cross lost his nerve and was unable to do the calculations. Pierrepoint stepped into the breach, did the sums, and told him exactly what the drop should be. The following day the execution went ahead without any problems. Shortly afterwards Pierrepoint's name was put on the list of chief executioners.

CHAPTER TWO

Anne

On 29 August 1943, at the age of thirty-eight, Pierrepoint married Anne Fletcher at St Wilfrid's Church, Newton Heath. Anne was the girl next door; she managed the sweet shop two doors down from the grocery where Pierrepoint worked. She is introduced in Pierrepoint's autobiography with three simple adjectives, rather like an advertisement for a new shampoo: 'blonde, gentle and practical'. Pierrepoint courted Anne for five years, a long time for a couple who were both in their thirties when they first met. In his autobiography Pierrepoint paints a quaint picture of this protracted courtship. Soon after they met Anne joined the Nursing Reserve and worked long hours away from home, so their moments together were few and precious. Pierrepoint bought his first car, a wire-wheeled Ford 8, the one and only time he paid for anything on hire purchase, and, on the rare occasions when she was not nursing and he was not delivering groceries (or assisting at hangings), they would motor over to Uncle Tom and Aunt Lizzie for freshly baked bread and homely chatter.

By this time Pierrepoint and Ivy were the only two children still living at home with their mother; Mary Pierrepoint and Ivy approved of Anne, but it was only after they had both died that Pierrepoint finally plucked up the courage to ask Anne to marry him. He describes how, through thrift, hard work and abstention, he managed to save a hundred pounds for the marriage. In his account he and Anne are the epitome of the respectable working classes: after the wedding they celebrated at the Mowbray Conservative Club and everyone sang 'God Save the King' before the newly-weds set off for their honeymoon in Blackpool. There was just one small snag: Pierrepoint hadn't told Anne that she had married the chief executioner.

Pierrepoint appears to be quite candid about this; he admits that he was scared to propose to Anne because he thought she wouldn't want to marry an executioner and he says that although he didn't spell it out to her before they married, he was confident that she knew what he did – Pierrepoint was not a common name and the town was a close-knit community. After their return from the honeymoon in Blackpool he was asked to do a job in Wandsworth. He packed his bag and told Anne that he would be away for a night. He didn't give her any explanation for his absence and, according to Pierrepoint, she didn't ask for one. A few weeks later he got a telegram from the Home Office asking him to come to London. Again he said nothing to Anne.

On his arrival in London he was told that the Home Office wanted him to fly to Gibraltar that night to execute two saboteurs. He was forbidden to speak about it for security reasons, so he wired Anne and simply said that he would be away for a few days. He was flown from Bristol airport to Lisbon on a specially designated route. It was a great moment for Pierrepoint: he was taking his first trip abroad on a dangerous, secret mission for his country. He says that on his return he told Anne everything. She was not surprised – she had known it all along, but she had been waiting for him to tell her about it himself. He goes on to explain that in the early days of the marriage he did not anticipate the degree of public attention that they were both subjected to in the years to come: 'I can only say that Anne has sailed through every storm as unaffected as a queen of the seas. She has still never asked a question. I have still never discussed my experiences with her. We have lived in mutual respect, as well as love.'

Albert and Anne, 'who in forty years never asked a question'

So, we have a rather neat and touching conclusion to the whole mucky business: Pierrepoint's discretion is intact, and Anne, swiftly transformed from a shampoo into a ship, sails on with dignity. We can picture the Pierrepoints, motionless with their cups of tea, frozen in time amidst the anaglypta and the poignant silence, quietly buttoned into the Edwardian strait-jackets that have kept their deeper, darker impulses at bay since childhood. We might wonder at the silence, but we can explain it away by referring to the times, imagining that Anne is content in her cardigan (after all, she cannot have aspired to happiness or fulfilment because they hadn't been invented).

We are being asked to accept that this is what it meant to be English, northern and working class in the 1940s, when people believed in duty, dignity and, of course, silence. This version isn't untrue, but it reduces Anne to a symbol of saintly womanhood. Anne wasn't a saint, she was an ordinary woman who shared her life and her bed with a man whose job it was to kill. Anne married Pierrepoint in 1943; it is possible – just – to believe that she made do with dignified silence at the beginning. But Pierrepoint worked as an executioner for thirteen years after they were married and in that time he hanged more than 350 people. What did she do with all those ghosts?

Anne is a shadowy, smiling figure in this story. Pierrepoint's autobiography may be misleading; perhaps the waters were not quite as calm as he suggests and Anne was not always the queen of the seas, but everyone I have spoken to has similar memories of her. She was a lovely woman and a perfect wife, she minded about her hair, and she played bingo. Everyone agrees that she never asked her husband about his work. But Pierrepoint's suitcase was hidden underneath the bed that he shared with Anne, and I want to know what she really thought when her husband went off on a job. I feel ashamed of my own curiosity when I remember the words of Rebecca West, writing about the Nuremberg Trials: 'No wise person will write an unnecessary word about hanging, for fear of straying into the field of pornography. The strain of evil in us which, given privileges, can take pleasure in the destruction of others by pain and death, takes delight in dreams about hanging, which is the least dignified form of death. That delight emits the strongest of all the stinks that hang about the little bookshop in the back streets.' I don't *feel* any pleasure or delight in asking these questions about Anne, but perhaps I'm fooling myself. Are my questions simply an invitation to pornographic speculation?

One definition of pornographic is 'dealing in the obscene'. Obscene means highly offensive and morally repugnant. In England it was the job of the official executioner to hang people by the neck until they were dead. The act, in itself, was highly offensive; to the opponents of capital punishment it was also morally repugnant, but to the supporters of capital punishment it was morally justifiable. Pierrepoint dealt in the obscene, but he did it on behalf of the state, and therefore on behalf of the people. In order to understand the nature of this obscenity, it is necessary to describe precisely what it was that Pierrepoint did when he said goodbye to Anne and went off on a job.

Pierrepoint and his assistant arrived at the prison at four o'clock in the afternoon on the day before an execution. The prison officers told them the weight and the height of the condemned prisoner and they had a look at the prisoner through the 'Judas hole' in the cell door so that they could assess his physique. The execution chamber was usually next door to the condemned cell, so the prisoner had to be taken out of the cell while Pierrepoint tested the equipment. He used a sack that was roughly the same weight as the prisoner and he calculated the correct drop using a Home Office Table of Drops (length relating to weight) and his own experience. He had to adjust the length of the drop to allow for the prisoner's particular physical characteristics. A very muscular man would have needed a longer drop, while a tall but thin man might have needed a slightly shorter drop. The sack was left hanging overnight in order to stretch the rope.

At seven o'clock the next morning Pierrepoint went back to the execution chamber to make sure that the rope was positioned at the right height for the prisoner. He worked quietly so that the prisoner would not be disturbed; he did not know that the execution chamber was next door to his own cell until a few seconds before the execution. The execution chamber was a small room with large trapdoors set into the floor. The trapdoors in the floor had two hinged leaves that were bolted together on the underside. To one side of the doors there was a lever that looked rather like an old-fashioned signalman's lever. When this was released the bolts drew back and the trapdoor opened.

Just before eight o'clock the next morning Pierrepoint and his assistant waited outside the condemned cell. On a signal from the sheriff they entered, accompanied by two prison officers. Pierrepoint walked straight up to the prisoner, put his arms behind his back and tied his hands together with a leather strap. At this point the door connecting the cell to the execution chamber opened for the first time and Pierrepoint led the way into the chamber. The prisoner was taken onto the drop and held on a marked spot, so that his feet were positioned across the division in the trapdoors. The prison officers stood on either side of him, holding him up.

Pierrepoint took the white cotton cap out of his breast pocket and put it over the prisoner's head, like a hood. Then he placed the noose around the prisoner's neck, while the assistant tied his legs together. The noose was not knotted, but the rope ran through a metal eye. This metal eye had to be placed under the prisoner's left jawbone to ensure that his neck was thrown back and his spinal column was broken. Otherwise he would be strangled. When Pierrepoint was satisfied that everything was in order he removed the safety pin from the lever, released the lever and the trapdoors opened. The prisoner fell into the pit below. Pierrepoint boasted that in most prisons the interval between his entrance into the condemned cell and the opening of the trapdoors was a maximum of twelve seconds. It was generally acknowledged that he did the job quicker than anybody else.

The execution was witnessed by the sheriff, the medical officer and the governor of the prison. When it was over the medical officer went into the pit and examined the prisoner to make sure that he was dead. Until 1953 the prisoner was then left to hang for one hour. In 1953 the rules changed and the prisoner was taken down from the rope once the medical officer had confirmed that he was dead. In some prisons there was a post-mortem, and whether or not this happened depended on the decision of the coroner. Pierrepoint placed the prisoner's body on a stretcher, ready for the post-mortem, or in a coffin, ready for the burial, depending upon the practice of the prison. He described this moment in his autobiography: 'A newly dead body is supple flesh, responsive to your handling and mutely asking your respect … The gentleness must remain.'

During the 1940s and 1950s the Coroner for North London carried out a post-mortem after every execution in Pentonville prison. He produced a schedule which showed that from 1943 onwards the spinal column had almost always been broken in the same place. He believed that dislocation at this point in the spine must have led to instantaneous death. The Coroner attributed this to the good advice of the pathologist on the required length of the drop. Pierrepoint had a different explanation: he believed that these perfect executions were the result of his own expertise.

An inquest was held immediately after the execution, inside the prison, and the prisoner was buried in the prison graveyard while the other prisoners were having their lunch. By the 1950s the prison graveyards were getting too full and in some prisons the bodies were being buried three deep. After the burial, two notices of execution and one coroner's inquisition notice were posted outside the prison gates. Pierrepoint did not attend the inquest or the burial; once the coroner had taken charge his job was over. He went home and waited for his cheque to arrive.

So that was it: Pierrepoint was paid to walk inside a prison, look someone in the eye, put a rope around their neck, and kill them. He did it for other people, because they couldn't, or wouldn't, do it themselves. He did it for the police and the judges and the Home Secretaries, but he also did it for millions of ordinary people. Until capital punishment was abolished in 1965, everyone in the United Kingdom lived alongside this obscenity. It was part of the fabric of life, whether or not you agreed with it. It was part of my parents' lives, part of the first two years of my own life. The opponents of capital punishment were a vociferous minority – most people supported it. Successive governments colluded with the public and together they accommodated this obscenity. It was a quintessentially English arrangement: the obscenity could be tolerated because it was concealed. The act itself was concealed behind the walls of the prison and the individual who committed the act was hidden behind his public persona.

Discretion was the key to this arrangement, and it worked both ways. The government depended upon the discretion of the executioner, and so, too, did the people, because the truth was too terrible to tolerate. The executioner, in turn, depended upon the discretion of the government and the people. If they asked too many questions, it would be hard to keep up appearances. So yes, these questions about Anne *are* pornographic, but not in the way that Rebecca West describes. They are pornographic because they deal with the obscenity, instead of concealing it. They are pornographic because they force a closer relationship with the obscenity. What is it like to share your life, and your bed, with a man who has hanged hundreds of people? The question is crude, salacious and voyeuristic. It conjures up a visceral horror and a feeling of shame. The question is also pornographic, and it is pornographic because it goes behind the discretion and the hairdos, behind the tactful silence and the lovely wife. It forces us to remember the existence of an ordinary woman, a woman to whom this question could be addressed. An ordinary woman and her husband, one living with violent death, the other inflicting it, year after year, acting on behalf of the government and the people. That is the obscenity.

CHAPTER THREE

Koestler and the Spies

On 3 September 1940 two small rowing boats came ashore on that unforgiving stretch of the Kentish coast between Hythe and Dungeness. Behind the beach lay Romney Marsh. It was about three o'clock in the morning, too dark to see clearly the faces of the young men who dragged the boats up the pebble beach and hid them in the grasses and reeds beyond. Each boat contained two men and they came ashore a few miles apart, one near Dymchurch, the other close to Lydd-on-Sea. The men had been towed by German minesweepers to within a couple of miles of the coast and from there they had rowed towards Dungeness. The coastline was being closely patrolled and by the beginning of September the patrols had reason to be particularly watchful: after months of preparation and uncertainty, the invasion now seemed imminent. In a secret session of Parliament on the night of 17 September Churchill told MPs that more than 1,700 barges and 200 ships were gathered at the ports under German occupation: 'At any moment a major assault may be launched upon this island.'

Private Tollervey was one of the soldiers charged with patrolling Romney Marsh on 3 September 1940. At about five o'clock in the morning he spotted a man in civilian clothes running towards the sea, coming from the direction of the marsh. He stopped him and asked him what he was doing. The man was ready with his answer: 'I have come across the water. I am a Dutch refugee.' He was taken for questioning and the soldiers started to search the marsh. They found a small rowing boat – the 'St Joan' – a suitcase full of men's clothes and a large sack of food. About half an hour later, in the same area, another man was stopped as he crossed a field behind the beach. Later in the day the search party was sent out again, with instructions to delve deeper into the hidden places of the marsh. Finally they found what they were looking for: hidden in a ditch, covered by the rushes, were two black leather cases. Each case contained the essential parts of a wireless set capable of transmitting messages across the Channel. The first man was Charles Albert van den Kieboom, a twenty-six-year-old Dutch citizen with a Dutch father and a Japanese mother. The second man was Sjoerd Pons, a twenty-eight-year-old Dutchman.

Later the same morning, in Lydd-on-Sea, Mrs Cow was serving behind the bar of the local pub when a young man came in and asked her for some cider to take away. She had never seen him before and it was very unusual for strangers to venture into militarily restricted areas like Lydd. The man spoke good English with a slight accent; Mrs Cow thought he might be a Canadian. There was another customer in the pub at the time, a civilian aircraft examiner, and the stranger aroused his suspicions. He followed him when he left the pub and watched him from a distance. The young man went to the grocery store and bought a packet of cream crackers and then he headed out of the village. At this point the aircraft examiner stopped him and demanded to see his identity card. The man produced a Dutch passport and he was immediately handed over to the police. The following day a fourth man was arrested near Lydd and another identical set of black leather cases were discovered shortly after his arrest. The man in the pub was twenty-three-year-old Karl Meier, a naturalised Dutchman who was born in Koblenz, Germany. The fourth man was Jose Waldberg, twenty-five years old, born in Mainz, Germany.

All four men had been sent by the German secret service, *Abwehr*, to gather information about the coastal defences and the movement of troops from Dungeness to Ashford and then on to London, information that might influence the strategic planning of the German invasion. Meier, who spoke excellent English, was also supposed to mingle with the locals, go to the cafés, listen to the soldiers and make friends. It was all strangely amateurish; Waldberg, who was the only one of the four with any experience of espionage, did not speak a word of English and it is hard to envisage how he could have operated effectively, forced to skulk around the south of England in mute disguise. They had all been told that the Germans would be arriving imminently, but there seemed to be no contingency plans and none of them knew how they were going to survive if the Germans did not arrive on schedule. (When Waldberg was captured he seemed to believe that the invasion had begun and he asked to be taken to the nearest German staff officer.) Nor did they have any idea of what might happen to them if they were captured; Waldberg had been told, and seemed to believe, that he would be treated as a prisoner of war. The men had been supplied with a suitcase of clothes and toiletries, a food sack and, most important of all, a raincoat. After their arrest the food sacks were seized and someone in MI5 made a list of the contents of each one: '10 tins of pork and beans, packed in Belgium.

18 tins of corned beef, American. 14 packets of eating chocolate, approximately 1lb each, all Belgian made. 12 2oz round packets of biscuits in a bag. 2 tins condensed milk, British made. 5 packets of Belgian cigarettes. 1 bottle of Cognac brandy.'

According to Meier's story, Meier and Waldberg had been captured because Waldberg was thirsty. They had left their food sack near the beach when they came ashore and it had been too dangerous to go back for it in daylight so they had been stranded without food or drink. Waldberg had developed a terrible thirst and Meier had been sent off to Lydd on a quest for food and drink.

The men were interviewed at Seabrook police station before being sent to Camp 020, MI5's wartime interrogation centre near Ham Common. Pons and Kieboom both told a similar story, suggesting that they had come to England under duress. Carl Meier didn't make any excuses. He said that he had been unemployed in Holland and that he had agreed to work for the Germans because he would be well paid. He went to Brussels where he was trained in Morse code and the structure of the British army: 'We put up in the Hotel Metropole. We stayed there for about a week and we were very lavishly entertained.' According to Meier, it was all rather jolly. The four men had set off on their mission from Le Touquet: 'We had a merry party just before we started out … They took a picture of us. They gave us our last instructions there.' Confusingly, he also said that he had only come to England because he thought that it would be the best way of getting to America. He had visited his American girlfriend in 1939 and now he wanted to return to America to get married. The initial interviews with Pons, Kieboom and Meier were all conducted in English and they were all cautioned at the start of the interview:

Interviewer: Before I go any further it is my duty to warn you that anything you may say will be taken down by this officer … and may on a future occasion be used in evidence.
Meier: It may be used against me?
Interviewer: No, it may be given in evidence in your favour or against you. You understand? English law is very fair.
Meier: I understand.

The fourth man, Jose Waldberg, was interviewed in German and French. He made no excuses for his conduct and he told the interviewer that he had been working for the German secret service as a professional spy for the last two years. These men were in fact the very first of a group of spies who came to be known to MI5 as the 'Invasion Spies'. They came over in small boats, parachutes, sea planes and U-boats, all of them badly trained and ill informed, believing that the German invasion, known as 'Operation Sealion', was imminent, all of them expecting support from the invading troops. Between September and November 1940 the *Abwehr* sent twenty-one spies to Britain to report on the defensive measures and the morale of the British people. The plan was known as 'Operation Lena' and many of the agents were working under duress. All but one of these agents were captured and the one man who avoided arrest eventually committed suicide in an air-raid shelter in Cambridgeshire in April 1941.

At Camp 020 Kieboom was instructed by the interrogating officers to transmit a message to Germany reporting that Pons had been shot and the rest of the group had gone into hiding. Under persistent interrogation the men gave MI5 names of potential agents and their contacts in England and details about the German secret service. On 7 September, four days after the arrival of these 'Lena' spies, hundreds of German bombers raided the East End of London. West Ham, Bermondsey, Poplar, Shoreditch, Whitechapel and Stepney were all devastated by the raids. The fire in the Surrey docks could be seen thirty miles away and the local fire officer was desperate: 'Send all the bloody pumps you've got; the whole bloody world's on fire.' The Blitz had begun. On the night of 15 October, with no cloud cover and a full moon, 410 raiders dropped 538 tons of high-explosive bombs, killing 400 people. Nine days later the four men who had been arrested in Kent were discharged from Camp 020 and handed over to the Civil Power. They were charged under Section One of the new Treachery Act, which had been given the Royal Assent just four months earlier. A person convicted of an offence under Section One of the Treachery Act was subject to a mandatory death sentence.

On 19 November 1940 Pons, Kieboom, Meier and Waldberg stood trial at the Old Bailey. It was the first prosecution under the new Treachery Act. Everyone in court – the barristers, the judge, the jury and the prisoners themselves – had been affected by the last three months of relentless bombing. The prisons where the four men were being held had been hit by German bombs and the trial itself was interrupted several times by the air-raid sirens. The hearing was held in camera and Mr Justice Wrottesley instructed the jury not to talk to anyone about the evidence that they were going to hear. Waldberg entered a plea of guilty at the outset and the trial of the other three men took four days. Pons and Kieboom were represented by Christmas Humphreys and Meier was represented by Gerald Howard.

When the jury had heard all the evidence, it was the turn of Mr Howard to address the jury on behalf of Carl Meier. It cannot have been an easy speech to make:

> You may think that this trial taking place here is a great tribute to the stability and balance of this country, a trial in its whole form and proceedings just as fair as the trial of any Englishman standing charged with any offence, and I know that is the spirit in which each one of you will consider this matter – a matter which is, as the learned Solicitor General told you in the opening, as solemn and grave as any you are ever likely to be called upon to consider. I know the spirit in which you approach that task will be just and fair as the form and letter of the proceedings. Gentlemen of the jury, it is not an easy task as you well know, in the middle of a war in which this country is fighting for its life against a formidable and ferocious enemy, at a time, as the sirens have twice reminded you this morning, when you and indeed all of us are in daily danger at the hands of that enemy, when you are asked to pass judgement upon a man who, on the evidence, has worked for that enemy, and on the evidence came to this country in the company of a self-confessed agent of that enemy. It is not an easy task to judge of that man in these times coolly and calmly, but gentlemen, because you are Englishmen, because you have been born and brought up in a tradition of freedom and fair play, I know that when the time comes you will accord to

> that Dutchman in the dock just the same scrupulous fairness that you would give to one of your own countrymen who was standing in the same place.

The Solicitor General was equally Churchillian in his closing speech for the prosecution:

> At least you will be convinced of this, that everything that could possibly be said for these men has been said … although the Germans may bomb this building brick by brick they will never succeed in destroying the heritage we have handed down to us and will hand on of British justice and British fairness. All I ask you to do is … to carry out your duty without fear or favour, without prejudice, but do not shrink from your duty because it is an unpleasant duty. Many of us today, and many of our young men today, have duties from which they might shrink, but thank God they do not shrink, and you will not shrink to do your duty as you see it.

The crux of the defence case was that the defendants had never intended to help the enemy. Christmas Humphreys had made a good case on behalf of Pons in particular, suggesting that he had never intended to spy, just to give himself up, but that he was afraid to give himself up with the wireless set so he planned to hide it first. He was arrested while he was hiding it, before he had a chance to turn himself in. Pons had a better case because, unlike the others, he had not said anything in his first interview that contradicted his defence. But Mr Justice Wrottesley was not impressed with Pons' explanation, nor, it seems, with all the rhetoric about fairness and the British justice system. In his summing up he dealt with Pons' defence quite succinctly: 'You may think that that is merely a cock and bull story. It is for you, you know, using the ordinary standards of common sense.' The jury retired and the three defendants waited for more than an hour and a half before they returned with their verdict. Meier and Kieboom were convicted. Pons was acquitted. This was the man who belonged to a group of enemy agents about whom Lieutenant-Colonel R.W.G Stephens, Commandant of Camp 020, wrote: 'What they lacked in preparation they made up in Nazi faith.' It was an amazing verdict; perhaps a credit to the advocacy of Christmas Humphreys, perhaps a credit to the much vaunted fairness of the system. MI5 was furious and so, presumably, was Mr Justice Wrottesley. Pons was immediately re-arrested under the Aliens Order, detained in Camp 020 during the war and deported to Holland when it was over.

Meier, Waldberg and Kieboom were sentenced on 22 November: ' The sentence of the Court upon you is that you be taken from this place to a lawful prison and thence to a place of execution, and that you there suffer death by hanging; and that your body be afterwards buried within the precincts of the prison in which you shall have been confined before your execution. And may the Lord have mercy on your soul. Amen.'

There was no appeal, but the men sought a reprieve from the Home Secretary. In his petition for clemency, Jose Waldberg claimed that he had come to England using a false identity. He was not Jose Waldberg at all, but Henri Lassudry, a dairyman, from Beaumont in Belgium. After the occupation of Belgium, his father had assaulted a member of the SS and Henri had been arrested by the Germans and forced into working for them so that his father would avoid punishment. MI5 were dismissive of this claim; in their view it was simply a desperate last-minute attempt to get a reprieve. The petitions were unsuccessful and it was announced that Meier and Waldberg would be executed on 10 December. Kieboom was scheduled to die a week later. The Sheriff wrote to Pierrepoint to ask him to act as assistant hangman for the execution of Meier and Waldberg. He had already assisted at more than twenty executions and they needed a trustworthy assistant for a double execution.

On 8 December 1940, as Pierrepoint was getting ready to come to London, the prison officers in Pentonville were preparing the prisoners for the execution. Meier and Waldberg were both given a pen and paper and the chance to write to their families. Meier wrote to his fiancée in America, a Miss Margaret S. Moseley of Ridge Avenue, Greencastle. The letter was written in almost perfect English:

> Darling,
> This is going to be the hardest letter I've ever written to anybody. You'll probably wonder what happened, but seeing that this letter is coming to you from England, I think you can guess why I'm here. It would be of no use to send you a letter explaining everything at the moment, as it will never pass the censor. I intend, however, to write a more detailed letter, than this one can possibly be. I will trust that one to the hands of the chaplain, who really is a very nice fellow and who will forward it to you after the war is over … Tuesday December the 10th at 9 a.m. will be a date of odious finality to all the optimistic hopes we cherished together in regards to our future life.

Perhaps I was meant to live only till I had conquered my cowardice, that even you, in spite of your love for me, must have known

For the first time in my life I've been able to set my jaws, clench my fists and say: 'life or death, I will live up to my ideal, so help me God!' It has made me free that realisation that I have finally conquered myself … I went into this with both my eyes open, telling myself that a man who has an ideal must be willing to sacrifice everything for it or else the ideal isn't an ideal at all, or the man is no man at all, but a manlike creature who deserves only pity … On the small amount of paper I'm allowed, I could hardly tell you all that I want to tell you, make it clear to you, how much I've appreciated everything you've done for me. I'm so glad that you always seemed to realise that my philandering had nothing at all to do with my love for you and I hope you'll posthumously forgive me for the pains it may have inflicted on you. Never have I more keenly realised, how much I love you than just these days. Only when I thought of you and of mother have I felt sorry, only then did I have to fight my tears back.

Margaret, you still have your whole life before you, there can be much happiness in store for you. There will be if you keep your mind open for it. Even this will pass and somehow I feel that we will meet again sometime somewhere else.

I'm therefore not asking you to forget me, but only to take care not to attach to [*sic*] much importance to the fact that I ever lived. I don't want to feel that my

> death will have ruined your life. I want you to get as much happiness out of your life as you possibly can …
>
> Darling, keep your chin up! Say goodbye to all our friends from me and here's all the love that my last thoughts will convey. I'm not going to say goodbye, because there must be something after this.
>
> Darling xxxx … So long!
>
> Carl

Carl Meier was twenty-four years old when he wrote this. He had been brought up in Germany by a German father and a Dutch mother. He was well educated; after school he had studied medicine, but he gave up before he was qualified and began to drift. Was it because he fell in love with Margaret? Was it too much philandering? Or something else entirely? He met Margaret when he was twenty years old and he visited her in America in 1939, before the war started. At some point he joined the Dutch Nazi party. Did he really believe that he was fighting for a great ideal? Was this young man's voyage across the Channel really his rite of passage, his journey into meaningful manhood? When he set out from Le Touquet, after that merry party, did he ever suspect that he was being sent on an ill-conceived, foolhardy mission? That he would most likely be shot, and that if he was not shot, he would be hanged? Hopefully, for Carl Meier's sake, he did believe in his own rhetoric. Hopefully, too, he believed that Margaret would read his letter, and that in reading it she would be his witness, the one person who could make some sense out of his death.

Carl Meier wrote one other letter on 8 December, to his mother in Maastricht. This letter was written in German. At the end of the letter he said goodbye:

> Little Mother – keep your head up. I shall be all the more proud of you.
> Receive a last kiss from
> Your son,
> Carl

The letters that Carl Meier wrote on 8 December in Pentonville prison were never sent. They are still sitting in a file in the National Archives in Kew. Perhaps the Home Office decided to keep the originals and sent copies, with any cuts that were required by the censor. It's a nice idea, but it seems unlikely. The situation was complicated because Meier was associated with Waldberg, and Waldberg had written three letters on 8 December. His letters were rather troublesome for the Home Office, partly because they were critical of the British legal system (Waldberg complained that he had not been given a fair hearing and that he had been told that if he pleaded guilty he would be granted a reprieve by the Home Secretary), and partly because there was some confusion about who the letters were from. The letter to his parents was addressed to Monsieur and Madame Lassudry:

> You know, father, how brave the little Belgians are when it comes to a fight, and you will be able to say of your poor son Henri that he died with the same noble courage … Goodbye for ever, from your son who loves you. Henri.

The letter to his uncle and aunt was addressed to Monsieur and Madame Lassudry Pierre:

> Forgive those who have sentenced me, forgive their

> great error … I will show them that a Belgian knows how to die … Your nephew who loves you, Henri.

Did Waldberg write these letters in his false persona, knowing that they would be read by the Home Office, as a final, desperate ploy to persuade the Home Secretary to grant a reprieve? Or was he really a poor dairyman from Belgium, condemned to another man's death? In the third letter, to his fiancée, Helene, he makes no mention of brave Belgians, nor of the reasons for his arrest:

> I end this terrible news, little Helene of my heart, sending you my last, my sweetest and most loving thoughts and most fervent kisses. Goodbye my darling, we shall meet again one day.
> The one who loves you to distraction
> Jose

There is nothing on the file in the National Archives that helps with this strange confusion. A memo from MI5 dated 9 December – the day after the letters were written and the day before the execution – dismisses Waldberg's claim to be Lassudry: 'No credence … can be given to this assertion, which is considered to be merely an afterthought in the hope of obtaining a reprieve.' Waldberg was going to be executed, whoever he was.

A week after the execution the Home Office wrote to Colonel Hinchley Cooke, who was in charge of the case, asking for translations and hinting at the difficulties: 'Waldberg … while testifying to the good treatment he received in prison, complains that English Justice failed him at his trial. He alleges that inter alia, he was deceived into pleading guilty and that his trial only took three minutes. These passages would prejudice the letters from our point of view, if there is any question of forwarding them to their destination.' Colonel Cooke did not respond and on 15 January 1941 the Home Office wrote to him again with a gentle reminder that the fate of the letters was still undecided. There was no reply.

On the morning of 10 December, as Pierrepoint and Stanley Cross ate their breakfast and checked their equipment for the last time, the whole prison was tensing itself for the execution: 'We all knew that somebody was going to be executed. The early morning timetable had been changed. Doors were closed quietly, not with the usual banging and clashing. Warders went about on tip-toe, with long faces. The entire prison became a house of death.' These are the words of a thirty-five-year-old Hungarian internee who spent six weeks in Pentonville in the winter of 1940. His name was Arthur Koestler.

Later Koestler played a crucial part in the campaign to abolish capital punishment and Pierrepoint became a target of his abolitionist polemic, *Reflections on Hanging*, but in 1940 Koestler knew nothing about the executioner who went to work in the execution chamber in Pentonville. Koestler and Pierrepoint were born in the same year, but there the pleasing symmetry ends; it is hard to imagine two places separated by a wider cultural divide than Budapest and Clayton, Yorkshire. Koestler was born in 1905, the only child in a solidly bourgeois home. His mother came from a distinguished Jewish family, originally from Prague, and she had spent a gilded youth in Vienna before the collapse of the family business forced her to move to Budapest. Koestler's father was a Hungarian businessman who ran a successful textile company until the outbreak of the First

World War, when the family was forced to move frequently between Budapest and Vienna, living in boarding houses. Koestler described his childhood in his autobiography. It is a far cry from Pierrepoint's rosy romp: 'I was an only child and a lonely child; precocious, neurotic, admired for my brains and detested for my character by teachers and schoolfellows alike.'

After a brief but passionate affair with Zionism, Koestler became the Middle Eastern correspondent for a German newspaper and by 1930 he had established a formidable reputation as a journalist and an editor. He arrived in Berlin on 14 September 1930, the day of the Reichstag elections when the National Socialists increased their vote by 80 per cent. Koestler, like so many intellectuals of the time, was thoroughly disillusioned and support for the Communists seemed to him the only effective way to oppose Fascism. In 1932, the same year that Pierrepoint's name was added to the official list of executioners and he became eligible to work as an assistant executioner, Arthur Koestler joined the Communist Party. For a few months he worked undercover for the Comintern, passing on any confidential information that came his way as foreign editor of a leading newspaper, before he was discovered and discreetly dismissed.

In the summer of 1932 Koestler was contracted by a literary agency to write a series of articles on the Five Year Plan, for distribution to a large number of European newspapers. His invitation to Russia was based on a secret agreement with the Party that these articles, supposedly written by a bourgeois liberal reporter, would describe a journey that convinced the reporter to overcome his prejudice against Communism. Koestler spent a year travelling through the Ukraine and Soviet Central Asia; there was a terrible famine and millions were starving – 'Women were lifting up their infants to the compartment windows – infants pitiful and terrifying with limbs like sticks, puffed bellies, big cadaverous heads lolling on thin necks' – but Koestler was still blinded by his political faith. He believed that the famine was inevitable and that the terrible conditions in Russia were an indictment not of Communism but of the backwardness of the Russian people.

On 13 July 1936 General Franco led an army mutiny in Morocco and within days the Spanish Civil War had erupted. Koestler wanted to fight in the Spanish Republican Army, but the Comintern had other ideas: he had a Hungarian passport – he could go to Franco's headquarters in Seville as a journalist and collect information about the involvement of the Germans and Italians. Koestler went to Seville and narrowly escaped arrest by the Nationalists after one of the German newspaper correspondents recognised him. In January 1937 Koestler arrived in Malaga just as it was about to fall to the Nationalists. Knowing that the Nationalists had issued a warrant for his arrest the previous year, Koestler took a huge risk when he decided to stay in the city. This time he did not escape: the Nationalist soldiers raided the house where he was staying and arrested him.

Koestler was held in Malaga for four days, where he witnessed the appalling torture of other detainees. He then spent three months in the Central Prison of Seville, two of those months in solitary confinement. He was told that he had been condemned to death in his absence, although there was a chance that the sentence might be commuted to life imprisonment. Koestler was not allowed any contact with the outside world during his detention and to begin with he was not taken out of his cell for exercise. Instead, he watched the other prisoners playing football in the prison courtyard. Slowly he came to understand that dozens of the men whom he watched playing football were mysteriously disappearing:

> On the nights of the executions we heard the telephone ring at ten o'clock. We heard the warder on duty answer it. We heard him repeating at short intervals: 'ditto … ditto … ditto … ' We knew that the warder wrote down a name before every 'ditto'. But we did not know what names they were and we did not know whether ours was among them … Then at twelve or one we heard the shrill sound of the night bell. It was the priest and the firing squad. They always arrived together. Then began the opening of doors, the ringing of the sanctus bell, the praying of the priest, the cries for help and the shouts of 'Mother'. We lay on our beds and our teeth chattered.

More than 200 men were executed during the three months that Koestler was held in the Central Prison in Seville. On 14 May 1937, without warning or explanation, he was released. His estranged wife, Dorothy Ascher, had campaigned relentlessly for his release and hundreds of distinguished institutions and individuals had sent letters and telegrams of protest to Franco. The British Government had intervened on his behalf and eventually his imprisonment became too inconvenient and he was released in exchange for a Nationalist prisoner.

In 1938 Koestler resigned from the Communist Party, shattered by the atrocities he had witnessed in Republican Spain and by the news of the show trials in Moscow, and started writing *Darkness at Noon*, the story of an old revolutionary who is arrested for treason, signs a false confession and is executed for crimes he did not commit. Koestler posted the novel to his publishers in London on 1 May 1940, nine days before Germany attacked the Low Countries and began to move towards France. After a series of picaresque adventures in occupied France, Koestler arrived in Britain on 6 November 1940, two weeks before Carl Meier and Jose Waldberg were due to stand trial at the Old Bailey.

Koestler was arrested at Bristol airport, taken to Cannon Row police station and then on to Pentonville. Technically he was 'an alien refused permission to land', and he would have to be screened before he could be released from custody. He had influential friends in London, including Harold Nicolson, the Duchess of Athol and Gerald Barry, the editor of the *News Chronicle*, and they quickly interceded to reassure the Home Office that Koestler was genuinely anti-Fascist. While he was in Pentonville, listening to the air raids and waiting for the bureaucratic wheels to turn, Carl Meier and Jose Waldberg were convicted of treason and sentenced to death, and *Darkness at Noon* was published. Koestler did not mind Pentonville: 'If I should write a Baedeker of the prisons of Europe, I would mark it with three stars.' On the morning of 10 December 1940, as the prison became 'a house of death', Koestler was reminded of the months that he had spent in the Central Prison of Seville and of the horrors of the nocturnal executions. Koestler did not know who was going to be executed that morning, or indeed that it was two men, not one. That did not matter. What mattered was that it was an extraordinary event in the life of the prison. According to his biographer, Iain Hamilton, Koestler recorded the exceptional nature of the event: 'It made all the difference. It was, as a matter of fact, what this war was about.'

The execution of Carl Meier and Jose Waldberg took place at nine o'clock in the morning. The St Pancras coroner, Mr W. Bentley Purchase, carried out the inquest in camera and although the prison did post the notices of execution on their gates, the whole event was tightly controlled. The executions were reported very briefly and there was no mention of Pons in any of the reports; in the interests of security the press had been asked to restrict themselves to the information that had been given out in the official press release and not to interview any of the witnesses. Three days later Koestler was released from Pentonville and four days after that Charles van den Kieboom was executed at Wandsworth prison. By the following year Pierrepoint had been promoted to the position of chief executioner.

In 1941 Pierrepoint could not have predicted that within the next four years his role as chief executioner would undergo a radical transformation. The world changed, and with it the role of the executioner. What Pierrepoint was called upon to do on behalf of the state between 1945 and 1948 would have amazed and bewildered his father and his uncle. Pierrepoint found himself in a post-war, post-Holocaust world, a world where the executioner had a new role. The first person he executed in his new position belonged to the pre-war era (Antonio 'Babe' Mancini was a London gangster convicted of a lethal stabbing in a night-club, executed on 31 October 1941), and during his first four years as chief executioner Pierrepoint hanged more than a dozen Germans. The real change came at the end of the war; he didn't know it at the time, but Pierrepoint's world was transformed on 15 April 1945, the day that the British liberated Belsen.

CHAPTER FOUR

Belsen

> *Belsen … can never be described, because every language lacks the suitable words to depict its horror. It cannot be imagined because even the most pathological mind balks at such a picture.* Gisella Perl

This is an extract from the testimony of a Belsen survivor. In Britain, Belsen will always be associated with horrifying photographs of heaped corpses. It was the first concentration camp to be liberated by the British Army, who reached Belsen a few days after the Americans had liberated Buchenwald, the first camp to be liberated by the Western Allies. British journalists, photographers and film makers were able to report on what they had seen within days of the liberation. Their reports revealed the horrors of the camp in graphic detail and the British public was exposed to reports and images that were entirely unlike anything they had ever seen before. Majdanek had been liberated in July 1944 and Auschwitz in January 1945, but the Nazis had moved most of the prisoners before the Soviet forces arrived. In January 1945 there were only 2,000 prisoners left in Auschwitz and although there was evidence of the mass murder that had taken place, Western journalists were not given much opportunity to investigate; it took some years for the British to understand exactly how the eastern camps had functioned as centres of extermination.

Bergen-Belsen concentration camp was near Celle in north-west Germany and, unlike the eastern camps, it was liberated intact. On 15 April 1945 there were an estimated 60,000 prisoners alive in Belsen, all being held in the most appalling conditions, the vast majority starving and desperately ill. The conditions were so terrible and the prisoners so ill that thousands more died in the weeks following the liberation of the camp.

Despite the fact that it contained tens of thousands of dead and dying prisoners, Belsen was not an extermination camp, however. It was originally built to accommodate Jewish prisoners who were selected by the German government as being suitable for diplomatic exchange, although fewer than 400 prisoners were ever released as a result of a genuine exchange, and gradually Belsen became a concentration camp. By December 1944 the conditions in the camp had deteriorated and the prisoners' needs were entirely neglected. At this point a new commandant took over: SS Captain Josef Kramer, who had been transferred from Auschwitz. Kramer and his staff instituted a regime of barbaric violence, and the physical conditions became so appalling that disease took hold of the horrifically overcrowded camp. In the winter of 1944–5 Belsen received thousands of prisoners who had been moved from camps in the east as the Soviet forces advanced and had survived the death marches and the terrible conditions of the transports. The numbers in Belsen rose from 15,000 in December 1944 to 44,000 in March 1945. Typhus became rampant and the dead were left in piles around the camp. It was estimated that between January 1945 and 15 April 1945, when it was liberated, 35,000 people had died in Belsen.

Belsen was liberated intact because it had been surrendered to the British. The Allies were advancing rapidly towards the camp and the Germans decided not to use their troops to move the prisoners because of the risk of typhus infection. On 15 April the 63rd Anti-Tank Regiment of the Royal Artillery, under the command of Lieutenant Colonel Taylor, entered Belsen. Josef Kramer was present at the liberation and shortly afterwards he was arrested. The British Army estimated that when the camp was liberated there were 10,000 corpses lying in the open air, most of them naked and decomposing. All the journalists who saw the camps were confronted with the failure of language. This was expressed very simply by the American broadcaster Ed Murrow: 'For most of it I have no words.'

The reports from Belsen, Buchenwald and the other German camps liberated in the spring of 1945 dominated the news in Britain and they seemed to have had a profound effect on the public. The Allies were advancing towards Berlin and newspapers were very thin as a result of paper rationing, but editors gave the reports from the camps priority. The Mass-Observation diarists of the time noted that everyone was affected by the news: 'The horrors of the German prison camps have got people properly now. One hears nothing else talked about' (18 April 1945); 'Everybody everywhere in the tram, in the office, [is] talking about the German atrocities now being uncovered and really, our wildest imaginings couldn't have pictured things as bad as they are' (18 April 1945); 'After listening to a description of one of the camps a deathly, grim silence falls:

nobody can give expression to what they are feeling, horror, pity, anger, amazement and helplessness – I think they all feel the same' (21 April 1945).

Five months later, on 17 September 1945, in Luneburg, inside the British Zone of Occupation, SS Captain Josef Kramer and forty-four others stood trial before a British military court, accused of war crimes committed in Belsen and Auschwitz. The cavalry barracks in Luneburg had been taken over by the British and the courtroom itself was a former gymnasium. It was the first of hundreds of war crimes trials held in British military courts and it took place amidst the devastation and cataclysmic upheavals of post-war Germany. The railways were not operating, hundreds of bridges were unusable and half the telephone switchboards were not working. Millions of displaced Germans were without a home and millions were struggling to reach their homes. Seven million people were moving in different directions and in the British zone it was the Control Commission for Germany that was responsible for imposing some kind of order.

The Luneburg hearing in September 1945 was preceded by years of disagreement and indecision on the part of the Allied leaders about how to deal with war crimes. By 1944 they had decided to distinguish between ordinary war criminals and their leaders, and had agreed that minor criminals should be dealt with in national courts while the major criminals should be dealt with on an international level. But they had not decided exactly *how* to deal with them. In the spring of 1945 the War Office came under increasing pressure from the battlefield commanders who needed to know what they were supposed to do with suspected war criminals. Finally in June 1945 the Royal Warrant was published, and this provided regulations for the trial of war criminals in British military courts under existing international law. The definition of war crimes was narrow, limited to crimes committed in German occupied territory against Allied civilians or military personnel, and these British trials were quite separate from the International Military Tribunal that sat at Nuremberg between 1945 and 1949.

The court at Luneburg had to consider two charges – the first relating to Belsen and the second to Auschwitz. The defendants were charged with committing a war crime in one or both of these camps, which meant that they had personally killed or ill-treated an Allied national, or that they had been involved with killing or ill-treatment to a degree that made them responsible for it. The prosecution involved two camps because in the winter of 1944 a section of the SS from Auschwitz, led by Josef Kramer, had been transferred to Belsen. Most of the defendants had belonged to this section. The court consisted of five British officers and the defendants were represented by one Polish and eleven British regimental officers, who were barristers in civilian life. During the trial the defending officers requested the presence of Colonel Smith, who was a professor of international law at London University, and he became another defending officer. There were forty-five men and women in the dock. This was not Nuremberg and the defendants were not Nazi leaders or ideologues, they were ordinary Nazis who put the policies into practice. Josef Kramer was the most notorious of the SS officers on trial – he had been a concentration camp guard since 1933 and had worked in Dachau, Mauthausen and Natzweiler before he was put in charge of the gas chambers at Birkenau in the summer of 1944. Kramer was the commandant of Birkenau when 200,000 Hungarian Jews were gassed to death. In December 1944 he was transferred to Belsen, where he oversaw a regime of unfettered violence and criminal neglect that led to tens of thousands of deaths. Josef Kramer's defence was that he had never participated in any selections for the gas chambers in Auschwitz, and that in Belsen, far from being responsible for the conditions in the camp, he had in fact attempted to improve them. The other defendants included Dr Fritz Klein, who had been responsible for making selections for the gas chambers in Auschwitz, and Irma Grese, a twenty-one-year-old dairy maid from eastern Germany who had embraced the Nazi ideology with passion. Her duties in Auschwitz included ensuring that the women under her control were taken to the gas chambers in an orderly fashion. She treated the prisoners with total contempt and in both camps she carried out random killings and vicious attacks on individual prisoners. Irma Grese's defence was that the allegations against her were fabricated or grossly exaggerated and that she had not had any involvement with the selections for the gas chambers.

The court sat for fifty-four days. More than twenty former prisoners of Belsen and Auschwitz were called to give evidence, and the court read more than a hundred affidavits sworn by former prisoners who were unable to come to court, and listened to hours of legal argument. At the beginning of the trial counsel for the defence applied, unsuccessfully, to have the Belsen and Auschwitz cases dealt with in separate trials and at the conclusion of the evidence Professor Smith made lengthy submissions on behalf of the defendants that firstly, the crimes committed at Auschwitz and Belsen should not be treated as war crimes at all, and that in any event the defendants were not responsible for these crimes because they were acting under superior orders.

I have always imagined this trial, and the hundreds of British and Allied trials that followed, happening in black and white.

The photographs are black and white – they show the defendants sitting in rows, with large numbered cards hanging around their necks, and they show the defending officers sitting at benches with stylish desk lights. (There are no white United Nations helmets as there were at Nuremberg, just the dark uniforms of the British Army, and there are no headphones for simultaneous translations – the interpreters were in the courtroom.) It is as if these hearings were always in the past, even before they had happened. They are such a solid piece of history, so well parcelled, that I never cared to unwrap them in my imagination. Then I read the transcript of the Belsen trial; suddenly it became a real trial, happening in real time. And that was what seemed so extraordinary: the time, or more precisely, the lack of time. Belsen was liberated on 15 April 1945. Within weeks of the liberation war crimes teams went into the camp to find potential witnesses. The conditions were still horrific and the living were surrounded by death (by June the survivors were still dying at a rate of twenty a day). These war crimes investigators had with them photographs of the SS who had been arrested at Belsen, and when they found someone who could make a positive identification and was prepared to give evidence of specific atrocities, they took a statement from them. The people who made these statements had experienced something entirely beyond the realms of human understanding, had suffered a trauma so great that it would reverberate for generations to come; the people who were helping them – soldiers, doctors, nurses, war crimes investigators, lawyers – were themselves transformed by the experience.

Helen Bamber was twenty when she arrived in Belsen in the winter of 1945, working for the Jewish Relief Unit. By this time the main camp had been flattened and the survivors were housed in the former barracks of the German army base about a mile away. The trial was underway in Luneburg, but in Belsen people were still dying. It was almost as if, in Belsen, it might be easier to die than to live. Speaking to her biographer, Neil Belton, Helen Bamber remembered how death felt different: 'There was so much death; so much talk of death. I think that when memories came back, and the whole horror was open in a way that it was not when they were freezing and starving – I think that people didn't fight sometimes to live, when it all became clear.' But a lot of people in Belsen *did* fight to live, and they spoke to Helen Bamber about what had happened to them: 'Above all else there was the need to tell you *everything*, over and over again … There wasn't much crying at that time, it was much later that they began really to grieve; some people had got far beyond that and they might never again have been able to weep; it wasn't so much grief as a pouring out of some ghastly vomit like a kind of horror, it just came out in all directions.' Helen Bamber went on to work for Amnesty International, before founding The Medical Foundation for the Care of Victims of Torture.

Many of the witnesses were too ill or too traumatised to come to court and many had died before the trial began. When a witness could not give evidence the prosecution submitted their evidence to the court in the form of sworn affidavits; more than half of the prosecution evidence was in this form. Those who were healthy enough to give evidence did so in open court. There were no screens, no video links, no press restrictions. These people had to describe their experiences in agonising detail and they had to step into the well of the court and look directly at the defendants in order to identify them. Just five months after enduring torture and degradation of a degree and on a scale that no one had ever encountered before, they were exposed to the gaze of the world and to their torturers. They were amongst the first to speak, to engage in that struggle with language that would continue for decades. Over the next sixty years the testimony of these invisible survivors (for obvious reasons the faces of these witnesses rarely appear in the history books) would be woven into the fabric of our collective memory, becoming a part of the texture of things. But in Luneburg, in the autumn of 1945, it had never been heard before. More than twenty men and women stood in the court and spoke of what had happened to them, just as the other witnesses, the ones who were not in court, were speaking to Helen Bamber. The 'ghastly vomit' was deodorized by the rules of evidence and the rituals of the court, but underneath it was the same thing. Terrible things had happened and then they had stopped happening, but they were not in the past.

Like a hellish version of *Alice in Wonderland*, the court proceedings bore a striking resemblance to the proceedings of a real British military court, and yet they were entirely dissimilar. The first witness for the prosecution was Brigadier Hugh Llewelyn Glyn Hughes, CBE, DSO, MC, the Deputy Director of Medical Services with the 2nd Army. He was responsible for the medical relief of Belsen and he was asked to describe to the court what he had seen when he first arrived at the camp on 15 April. This is how he started his evidence: 'The conditions in the camp were really indescribable; no description nor photograph could really bring home the horrors that were there outside the huts, and the frightful scenes inside were much worse.' He went on to speak about the piles of corpses, the mass graves, the human excreta, the huts where the dead and the living were crowded together. He concluded his evidence in chief with this observation: 'I have been a doctor for thirty years and have seen all the horrors of war, but I have never seen anything to touch it.'

The second prosecution witness was Captain Derrick Sington of the Intelligence Corps, who was one of the first officers to go into Belsen on 15 April. Later the same day he had spoken to Kramer. He was asked by the prosecutor to describe Kramer's general attitude: 'In his office he sat back in his arm-chair, tilted his hat back, and was generally confident. He expressed no emotion about the camp.' How could these men be judged by the ordinary standards of the civilised world, a world that seemed to have disappeared? The answer, from the point of view of the British Army, was simple: justice had to be seen to be done and, by being seen to do justice, the court would be helping to rebuild that lost civilisation. So the legal machine from the old world rolled into action, fastidious and judicious to a degree that seemed absurd and essential in equal measures.

On the seventh day of the trial the court heard the evidence of Dora Szafran, a twenty-two-year-old Polish Jew from Warsaw. There was nothing unusual or remarkable about her evidence; it was typical, in fact. She had been taken to Majdanek in May 1943 and after seven weeks was transported to Auschwitz. In Auschwitz she had survived several selections and had witnessed the defendants Josef Kramer, Franz Hoessler and Dr Fritz Klein taking part in those selections. She arrived at Belsen in January 1945 and in her evidence she said that the conditions there were 'so bad that it is impossible to find words in this world. In half a barracks there were 600 to 700 people. We were lying on the floor covered with lice and every other kind of vermin one could imagine ... There was no bread for four weeks before the arrival of the British troops.' She worked from three o'clock in the morning until nine o'clock at night in the kitchens in order to have a bed and a little more soup.

In her evidence she described in some detail a particular incident at Auschwitz that involved one of the defendants, SS officer Juana Bormann:

> In 1943, when we were in Block 15 at Auschwitz, we were coming back from work and one from the Kommando had a swollen leg and could not keep up with us. Bormann set her dog on her. I think it was an Alsatian. First she egged the dog on and it pulled at the woman's clothes; then she was not satisfied with that and made the dog go for her throat. I had to turn away, and then Bormann proudly pointed out her work to an *Oberscharführer* [SS sergeant]. I saw a stretcher being brought along, and I should think she was just about alive. Bormann also took part in selections.
>
> *Q:* How were the selections made?
>
> *A:* They were made in such a manner that people with blemishes, weak and ill people, were chosen. Selections were, in fact, a form of liquidation. I lived in Block 25 and many times saw people taken to the crematorium. People were taken along from the hospital both by day and night. There were shouts and shrieks.

Bormann's barrister, Major Munro, rose to his feet to cross-examine the witness. (All the defence barristers represented more than one defendant and most of them represented four. For the officers acting on behalf of the defendants who were seriously implicated by the prosecution evidence, this was a heavy burden; Major Munro represented Franz Hoessler, Juana Bormann, Elisabeth Volkenrath and Herta Ehlert.) Major Munro carefully challenged Dora Szafran's evidence about the dog: 'Is it not the case that the dog escaped from the guard's control? Is it not the case that the woman who had charge of the dog tried to stop it from attacking the other woman?' And so on. As if it was an ordinary case, as if there had been no mention of the gas chambers and the selections. As if the courtroom was not steeped in death and ghastly vomit. Bormann's defence to the allegations made by several witnesses that she had repeatedly and deliberately urged her dog to attack prisoners in Auschwitz was, essentially, one of mistaken identity. She did have a dog, but her dog never attacked the prisoners. In relation to the selections, she simply said that she had never been present at a selection and that, again, the numerous witnesses who saw her were mistaken.

The transcript records Major Munro's closing speech on behalf of Bormann and the others: 'He pointed out to the court that when a girl has been arrested for no apparent reason, sent to a concentration camp, her father, mother and family sent to a gas chamber, and she herself had ended her captivity in the dreadful conditions at Belsen, it was not unnatural and not surprising she should come into court *revengeful*, possibly *vindictive* [my italics].' In an ordinary trial, this would have been a perfectly routine submission – if the victim has an axe to grind, please treat her evidence with caution. Major Munro was simply doing what he always did: putting the case for the defendant. He found himself in this hellish, parallel universe and, like Pierrepoint, he simply kept on doing his job. That was the whole point of being there.

On 13 November 1945 Colonel Backhouse made his closing

speech for the prosecution in the court in Luneburg. It was a good speech and an important speech, but it didn't make the headlines in Britain; people felt that the Luneburg trial had taken too long, and although the papers had initially been full of the horrifying revelations from the concentration camps (Kramer quickly became the 'Beast of Belsen'), the long legal arguments and the insistence on detail were a far cry from the summary justice that many had wanted. As early as 30 September a rather sarcastic report in *The Times* had expressed the ambivalence of the British attitude to the Luneburg trial: 'The wheels of the law are grinding exceedingly small in the Belsen trial, which enters upon its third week here … International observers, and certainly the Germans themselves, are no doubt impressed by the pains taken by the Court to extend all the privileges of British justice to the accused, who in other circumstances might have been dealt with more summarily.' A week later, according to *The Times*, the speed of the trial was becoming a serious concern: 'Both the Government and the War Crimes Commission are thought to be concerned at the length of the proceedings, and the effect on world opinion.' (From a modern perspective, the complaint about the speed of the trial seems absurd: when Slobodan Milosevic died he had been on trial in The Hague for four years.) Colonel Backhouse reminded the court of what the case was all about:

> Although Kramer would not admit it to me in cross-examination, when it was put to him in re-examination he said: 'It was a doctrine of my party to destroy the Jewish race.' Whatever other places may also have been used in the course of this destruction, in Auschwitz alone literally millions of people were

> gassed for no other reason than that they were Jews … Here something was going on which completely defeats the imagination.

Three days later the court delivered their verdict: of forty-four men and women in the dock at the end of the trial, thirty were convicted and the remaining fourteen acquitted. Nineteen of those convicted were given sentences of imprisonment ranging from life to one year. The remaining eleven, including Josef Kramer, Irma Grese, Fritz Klein, Franz Hoessler and Juana Bormann, were sentenced to death.

On 10 December 1945, three weeks after the death sentences had been passed, an official announcement was made from Field-Marshall Montgomery's headquarters: the appeals against the sentences had been rejected and the prisoners were to be hanged. This was an important moment for the British Government: the executions would demonstrate that British justice, which had been criticised for being slow and ponderous, could also be an effective instrument of retribution and even, perhaps, revenge. But of course this was British retribution. The publicity was a political necessity and it was designed to promote an *idea*, but the act itself had to be carried out behind closed doors – quickly, efficiently and with the utmost discretion. Pierrepoint got the job. Two days after the announcement Pierrepoint was flown from RAF Northolt to Buckeburg in Germany. He was given the rank of Lieutenant-Colonel, but he wore his usual suit and tie. At Northolt a crowd of reporters and photographers pursued him across the tarmac. Without any consultation, he was paraded in public and his discretion was trampled underfoot. For the first time in modern history, the hangman was officially embraced by the British state.

Pierrepoint arrived at Buckeburg on the evening of 11 December and he was met by a British officer. In the dark and the rain they were driven across the freezing ruined wastes of northern Germany to Hameln where the Luneburg prisoners were being held. Captain Derrick Sington later described the prison at Hameln:

> It lies close to the river. Behind the entrance portals and the studded gate is a shady tree in a sandy courtyard. The yellow stucco of the building has an almost baroque charm. Like others of its kind the outside of this prison belies its interior where cavernous corridors are rank with a foetid smell and where the desolation makes the heart contract. The tiny barred window in each cell is set high up in the wall as if even so little light were begrudged.

(Sington became an opponent of capital punishment and he described the execution of the Nazi war criminals as 'useless as well as barbaric'.)

There were a total of thirteen prisoners waiting to be hanged in Hameln – the eleven convicted at Luneburg and two others who had been convicted of the murder of a prisoner of war in Holland – and when Pierrepoint arrived he was told, for the first time, that he was expected to hang all of them in one day. This would be the largest mass execution in the history of British executions and the British Army were putting Pierrepoint in charge of the whole operation. Pierrepoint was billeted outside the prison and he went to bed late on the night of 11 December. He had thirty-two hours to prepare.

On 12 December Pierrepoint arrived early at the prison. The

way that he describes this moment in his autobiography is so ridiculous that it might just be true: he says that the prison gates were opened by a German prison officer who couldn't speak English. Pierrepoint couldn't speak any German and so he found himself stranded outside the prison, unable to explain the reason for his visit. He was rescued by Regimental Sergeant-Major O'Neill, a German-speaking member of the Control Commission, who had been seconded to work as Pierrepoint's assistant at Hameln. O'Neill was an excellent interpreter, but Pierrepoint was slightly horrified to learn that his assistant had never even witnessed an execution. He was soon reassured. O'Neill was a quick learner and a very able assistant and he went on to assist Pierrepoint in all his executions of Nazi war criminals.

Their first job on 12 December was to test the gallows which the Royal Engineers had just finished building according to specifications set down in a Home Office blueprint. As O'Neill led Pierrepoint through the prison they passed through the corridor of condemned cells where the Luneburg prisoners were held, and Pierrepoint immediately recognised the much photographed features of Josef Kramer, the 'Beast of Belsen'. In his autobiography Pierrepoint recalls that on their way to the gallows the silence of the prison was broken by a strange scraping sound which came from the prison yard. He looked out and saw a group of workmen digging thirteen graves. Concerned about the effect this might have on the condemned prisoners, Pierrepoint complained to a prison official. Nothing could be done: the ground was stony and frozen, and the graves had to be dug. Pierrepoint describes the pity that he felt for the condemned prisoners at Luneburg as he saw them watching him through the bars of their miserable cells. How strange that

Pierrepoint, who had been unmoved by the sight of so many condemned prisoners, most of them guilty of an isolated and unpremeditated act of violence, should experience a moment of empathy with men and women who had participated in mass murder on an unprecedented scale. Was his pity an expression of how the poor conditions in the prison had affronted his professional sensibility – was he sorry for them because they weren't in a British prison? Or was he moved by their numbers? Perhaps seeing thirteen men and women all awaiting death at the same time had revealed something new to him. Pierrepoint wants to tell his readers about his pity, but he also knows that it might be frowned upon. He spoke about his feelings to a group of British soldiers in the prison and they told him that if he had been into Belsen he would not be feeling sorry for the prisoners.

After testing the gallows Pierrepoint had to do something that he had never been asked to do before: he had to personally supervise the weighing and measuring of all the condemned prisoners. Pierrepoint needed to know the weight and height of each prisoner so that he could calculate the correct drop, but in British prisons the weighing and measuring was always done by prison officers before the executioner arrived, leaving the executioner to look through the 'Judas hole' in the cell door, unseen by the prisoner, to assess his musculature in order to fine-tune his calculations. The whole idea was that the condemned prisoner should not set eyes on the executioner until the moment when he walked into the cell on the morning of the execution: a thoughtful process, with a fine dramatic climax. But in Hameln there was no time and no appetite for these niceties; Pierrepoint and O'Neill had to set up a weighing scale and a measure at the far end of the condemned corridor. One by one the prisoners were taken from their cells, asked for their personal details –

name, age, religion – measured, and told to stand on the scales. O'Neill asked the questions and translated the answers so that Pierrepoint could make a note.

The last three prisoners were the women – Irma Grese, Elisabeth Volkenrath and Juana Bormann. Irma Grese's name was well known to Pierrepoint – just as the British press had seized on Josef Kramer's dark, thick-set features and dubbed him the 'Beast of Belsen', so Irma Grese, who was young and blonde, had been refashioned as a satanic tabloid pin-up. It wasn't just the popular press; the first edition of the Luneburg trial transcript was published in 1949 with a long and learned introduction by the editor, Raymond Phillips, MC, MA, BCL (Oxon.), Barrister-at-Law. In the midst of his commendably thorough introduction, Phillips is momentarily distracted by Irma Grese: 'Her appearance was certainly striking. She was handsome rather than beautiful. But with her youth, her blonde hair, broad forehead, firmly modelled nose, and blue defiant eyes she was one to remark.'

Derrick Sington, too, was struck by Grese: 'She was, by any standards, a pretty girl – the only one in the dock. Her hair was blonde, with fair ringlets resting on neat shoulders. Her eyes were clear blue under a high, broad forehead. She might have been a handsome young nurse, a secretary, or even the head prefect of a girls' school.' This re-invention of Grese as a child like object of male patronage and desire is a grim footnote to the Luneburg trial, and although Pierrepoint's recollection is less obviously lascivious, it is equally peculiar; he remembers that Grese was laughing as she came out of her cell and walked towards him: 'As bonny a girl as one could ever wish to meet.'

Pierrepoint spent the rest of the afternoon calculating the length of the drop for each prisoner. It was a difficult exercise and he was anxious not to make any mistakes; because of the numbers, he had to work out the order of executions and then make an allowance in his calculations for an adjustment of the rope after each execution. He knew that the prisoners would hear the drop from their cells and so he decided to take the women first, so that they would be spared a long wait. There would be three single executions of the women, followed by five double executions of the men. Before returning to his billet, he went through a rehearsal with Sergeant O'Neill, painfully aware of the prisoners in nearby cells.

At half past nine on the morning of 13 December Pierrepoint hanged the first of the thirteen prisoners, Elisabeth Volkenrath. The executions were witnessed by Brigadier Paton-Walsh, who was the Deputy Governor of Wandsworth prison, and Miss Wilson, Deputy Governor of Strangeways prison (the regulations required the presence of a female witness for the execution of a woman). By 10.38 a.m. all three women had been hanged, and Pierrepoint and O'Neill paused for a cup of tea. They resumed with the double hanging of Josef Kramer and Dr Fritz Klein, followed by Karl Francioh and Peter Weingartner. They stopped for lunch and then hanged the remaining four prisoners. By 4.30 in the afternoon all the condemned prisoners were dead and their bodies had been laid in the stony ground. That evening Pierrepoint was fêted at a mess party and presented with a memento of his first visit to Hameln – an engraved clock. He returned to Britain the following day, where he was besieged by journalists anxious to get a quote from Britain's avenging angel.

In 1946 Pierrepoint went to see Winston Churchill address a public meeting in Manchester. Many years later he spoke about the experience:

> I am often asked, 'What has been the most memorable occasion in your career?' I always reply that it was in 1946 in a crowded hall at Belle Vue when Winston Churchill was speaking ... After the rally I was invited back to a special room for guests only and had the honour and pleasure of shaking hands with the great Winston. His handshake was as strong as his character. I still have felt that handshake on many occasions, especially when I have felt under the weather.

Pierrepoint's trip to Hameln in December 1945 was the first of many. Sergeant-Major Morris, serving with the 4th Battalion of the Somerset Light Infantry, was responsible for looking after visitors of officer status and making sure they were given decent accommodation. He remembered one particular visitor to Hameln: 'I met the great Pierrepoint ... In this case it was an old hotel that had been turned into an officers' mess, an area for people like him, held in high esteem by the authorities.' Asked what Pierrepoint looked like, Morris chuckled: 'Well, to put it bluntly, a bit like a sort of butcher-type man. Red-faced, plumpish chap.' Pierrepoint's visits to Hameln didn't stop until 1949; in September 1947 he was given a second assistant for the multiple executions. Edwin Roper was forty-one years old when he first worked with Pierrepoint (a year younger than Pierrepoint himself) and he had spent the previous twelve years working as a chief executioner in Shanghai and Hong Kong.

Roper recalled with great pride his first job as assistant to Pierrepoint on a multiple execution of fourteen people: 'We found ourselves welded into a perfect team and working with machine gun precision. This cohesion was no doubt due to the identical methods adopted by both of us and the wealth of hanging experience which as Chief Executioners, we had both previously acquired.' (He conveniently forgot to mention Sergeant O'Neill, who had already assisted Pierrepoint on about a hundred executions by this time.) Roper held Pierrepoint in very high esteem:

> 'He is one of the finest men it has been my privilege to meet and I am confident that no better man could be found anywhere to occupy the position which he holds. He is methodical, acts very fast and endeavours to put the condemned man out of his misery as soon as is humanly possible. In fact, I think he almost regards it as his sacred duty. In private life he is a charming, hail-fellow, well-met character with a merry twinkle in his eye. I shall always look on him as a great personality – humble, kind and sincere ... By [February 1948] we were becoming known to the populace of Hamelin and would often hear remarks in the street of '*Der Henker, Der Henker*!'

In less than three years – between December 1945 and October 1948 – Pierrepoint hanged 226 people, always acting as chief executioner. One hundred and ninety-one of them were Nazi war criminals or Allied Nationals who had been convicted of war crimes by British military courts in Germany. This was something entirely different from the occasional hanging of a mobster in Pentonville or a jealous husband in Strangeways. Without warning, and without any official recognition of this new role, the executioner had become an instrument of national retribution on a massive scale. Pierrepoint's Uncle Tom was an executioner for forty years and in that time he carried out 294 executions, either as chief or assistant executioner. The executions in Germany were usually multiple ones and a total of at least ten people in one day became commonplace. Pierrepoint was sometimes asked to do two consecutive days of multiple executions, since this was the most economical way to use his services; on 16 and 17 May 1946 he executed a total of seventeen people. On 26 June 1947 he executed another thirteen prisoners and on 27 February 1948 he executed fifteen prisoners.

The carefully choreographed ritual of an execution in a British prison was abandoned under the pressure of time and numbers and Pierrepoint learnt to tolerate the summary procedures that had shocked him in December 1945. Although he admitted that he was disturbed and exhausted by the process, he claimed that he had no doubts about the morality of this new system. The belief that he had done everything he could to dignify the proceedings and to mitigate the suffering of the condemned prisoners kept him going. His faith in this self-imposed code of professional conduct was not a religious faith but it operated in the same way and was the key to his survival: it insulated him from doubt.

Pierrepoint did not receive any official recognition of his services in Germany. He says in his autobiography that the War Office had told him they were going to put his name forward for a commendation, but that he refused to be considered. For many years after the Luneburg executions he received an envelope each Christmas. Inside the envelope there was a five-pound note and a piece of paper. On the paper was written: 'BELSEN'. Pierrepoint never discovered the identity of the donor and after some years the envelopes stopped coming.

In 1946 Pierrepoint had left the grocery business and taken

over the lease of a pub in Hollinwood, near Manchester. He wanted to run his own business, mostly because it would make life easier when he needed time off for a job. (He was delighted to discover that he could carry out an execution in Dublin, catch the three o'clock plane and get back in time to open up at half past five.) The pub was a great success, partly due to Pierrepoint's new celebrity status. People wanted to come to the pub to see the hangman; the stories in the newspapers were an unpleasant intrusion into his private life, but they were good for business. According to the memoirs of Syd Dernley, an assistant executioner who worked regularly with Pierrepoint, these 'trippers' were a regular feature in Pierrepoint's pub: 'Some just sat with a drink and stared at Pierrepoint ... Some asked to shake hands with him – which he invariably did with a friendly smile.' Tommy Mann says that Pierrepoint was always interested in making money, perhaps because he never forgot the poverty of his childhood. Pierrepoint was very sociable and he relished his new incarnation as a twinkling, jovial figure behind the bar. And of course he was perfectly discreet; he was happy to shake hands, but claimed that he never indulged the curiosity of the more inquisitive trippers. According to Pierrepoint, his 'home team' were all models of discretion and they made sure that no one overstepped the mark: 'I was very touched to have their loyalty.' Pierrepoint did not rename the pub when he took over the lease. It was called Help the Poor Struggler.

Pierrepoint's new job made him more visible, and journalists were always looking for stories about his trips to Germany. On 27 August 1946 he wrote to the Prison Commissioners:

> I have had a good number of Press people round to see me, but under no circumstances would I entertain

> them. I have just learned that one of the Press has been to the Police, and my last place of employment, and friends, finding out all about me trying to piece a story together. I have now had a War-Correspondent specially to see me from London, saying he met me at Belsen, which I knew was wrong because I never went to Belsen. I was at Hameln. I refused to converse with him, he told me he had got my story but wanted me to o.k. it. I definitely refused to say anything. He left me saying I was stupid and [he] was going to put a big article in the *Sunday Pictorial* about me this week end. The reason for me writing to you is any article which now may appear in any paper, will definitely not have come from me.

The article did appear in the *Sunday Pictorial* in September 1946, while Pierrepoint was in Vienna. The minutes on the Prison Commission file are interesting:

> I think Pierrepoint's letter can be accepted … Nevertheless, there are a few general statements in the article which lead one to suppose that Pierrepoint has given certain information from time to time to his intimates, which has been passed on and is here presented in garbled form. I am of opinion, consequently, that it would not be possible to take any proceedings against Pierrepoint in respect of the article … Pierrepoint is at present in Vienna where he is employed by the Control Commission executing some Austrian criminals with a view to introducing the English method of execution into that country.

> He will probably proceed to Germany early next month.

Perhaps Pierrepoint's discretion had slipped a little, and perhaps his 'home team' was not quite as loyal as he imagined. It didn't make any difference – he was much too useful to be prosecuted.

Albert Pierrepoint, publican

In Help the Poor Struggler in the autumn of 1946 the gossip was that Pierrepoint would be going over to Germany to execute the Nuremberg war criminals. There had been speculation about this in the British newspapers, but in the event the hangman was an American, Master Sergeant John C. Woods, who was assisted by two GIs. To the dismay of the British Government, the Allied Control Council agreed to the American request that two members of the press from each of the four zonal governments should be present at the executions.

The British Government was right to be concerned – afterwards photographs of the executed corpses with blood on their faces were released to the press and there were claims that the executions had been hideously bungled and that the prisoners had died of slow strangulation. Just as the government had feared, the public had been given too much information and as a result the Allied Control Council had lost control of the spectacle.

It was an unedifying conclusion to a difficult sentencing process; the defendants convicted at Nuremberg had appealed against their sentences and the four-power Allied Control Council was the final court of appeal. Lord Douglas, who had taken over from Montgomery as the Commander-in-Chief and Military Governor of the British Zone of Germany and the head of the British element of the Allied Control Council, had what he described as the 'distasteful duty of sitting in judgement on these appeals'. In his memoirs he described his anger about what he perceived as political interference from Ernest Bevin, Secretary of State for Foreign Affairs, who wanted to ensure that the appeals were not successful. Douglas was particularly unhappy at having to reject Goering's appeal: 'Twenty-eight years before, Goering and I, as young fighter pilots, fought each other in the cleaner atmosphere of the air. As I spoke the words that meant for Goering an irrevocable death sentence I could not help feeling, for all my loathing of what he had become, the strongest revulsion that I should have to be one of those so directly concerned with it.' It seems that it was not only the death sentence itself that disturbed Lord Douglas, but in particular his *proximity* to it. 'At the end of the second day of the meeting in Berlin there was a discussion about the way in which the bodies should be cremated after the hangings, and how to dispose of the ashes … I have seldom, if ever, known a feeling of such acute distaste as that which I experienced when I found myself having to participate in this last macabre discussion.' Since Lord Douglas, along with the rest of the world, had just seen and heard evidence of the gassing of millions of Jews in the concentration camps, his feelings are, at first, a little puzzling. Perhaps it was that very English dislike of proximity again – it was simply in poor taste to get too close. The Lord Douglases of the world relied upon the Pierrepoints of the world to deal with the whole unpleasant business behind closed doors, quietly, and without any fuss. Nuremberg was not discreet.

CHAPTER FIVE

John Amery

On 19 December 1945, six days after he had returned from Hameln, Pierrepoint executed a thirty-two-year-old man called John Amery at Wandsworth prison. Like William Joyce ('Lord Haw-Haw'), who was also executed by Pierrepoint, Amery had been convicted of high treason after broadcasting from Berlin during the war. He was the son of the Conservative politician, Leo Amery, who had been at school with Winston Churchill and became Secretary of State for India in 1940, and Florence Greenwood, the sister of Liberal MP Hamar Greenwood. His childhood was spent in a large house in Eaton Square and, like his father before him, he was educated at Harrow. He had one younger brother, Julian Amery, who became a Conservative MP, but John Amery showed no interest in conforming or following his father's example. He was a wild boy right from the start: charming, seemingly clever, and utterly unpredictable. At Harrow he hated the discipline and challenged all the conventions; he stole from other boys and escaped at night to go into the West End. His housemaster was defeated by his behaviour: 'In the whole of my experience as a schoolmaster, I found him, without doubt, the most difficult boy I have ever tried to manage ... He seemed to revel in the fact that so many of his companions thought him mad. Rules and regulations, so far as he was concerned, did not exist, and as a consequence he was continually falling foul of masters and boys.' By the age of twenty he had been arrested for dangerous driving, contracted syphilis and turned down the place that had been offered to him at Oxford University. Leo Amery's diary entries for 1932 are shot through with anxiety for his eldest son:

> 22 August – Drove back ... to find ... cables, one from Jack to say that he proposed to get married that morning, not even mentioning to whom.
>
> 23 August – Rung up by *Evening News* from London to say that Jack and Miss Wing had gone off to Paris in the hope of getting married on the Continent somewhere (the latest news is that they are trying to do it on the Latvia-Soviet border!) ... I came to the conclusion that I could not risk leaving it to B. [his wife] to cope with the situations that might possibly arise, if Jack got into trouble on the Continent, or came back and made scenes, so I cancelled my engagements.

Miss Wing, described as an actress, was in fact a prostitute. She had no idea that the young man who wanted to marry her was only twenty years old and therefore could not do so without his parents' consent. Leo Amery did not consent but he did give his son financial support. John Amery and Miss Wing travelled across Europe, ending up in Greece. Two weeks before his twenty-first birthday Amery converted to the Greek Orthodox

Church and got married in Athens without his parents' consent. His behaviour became increasingly erratic and his lifestyle correspondingly extravagant. Leo Amery's diary describes the unfolding of a family tragedy:

> 31 December 1932 – So much for 1932 … Meanwhile I have tried to do something to mend a completely derelict financial situation and have scraped together an income which, but for Jack, might more or less see things through. Jack has cost us both much, of which money has been the smallest item. But Julian promises well and is growing in mind and stature.

In 1936 Amery was declared bankrupt and he spent more and more time travelling in Europe. In France he came under the influence of Jacques Doriot, founder of the Parti Populaire Français, which was rabidly fascist and anti-Semitic, and this marked the beginning of his enduring fascination with fascism. For four years he drifted across Europe, spending time in France, Spain and Italy, supported by his parents and his own shady dealings, and when Germany invaded France on 10 May 1940 and his father became a member of Churchill's cabinet, Amery was stuck in Vichy France. His curious twilight life continued until March 1942 when he wrote a letter to a French newspaper complaining about an RAF bombing raid on the Renault industrial complex in the suburbs of Paris, during which more than 600 French civilians had been killed. Criticism of the British Government in a newspaper that was controlled by the enemy was a serious offence, and when the letter came to the attention of the British Intelligence Services Amery's name was placed on the postal censorship blacklist, so that they could keep track of his contacts with England, and given to the port authorities in case he returned.

In the autumn of 1942 Amery went to Berlin for the first time to discuss the possibility of making broadcasts to the British; he was a fantasist and the attentions of the German Foreign Office fed his distorted sense of his own importance. The deal was that all his living expenses would be paid by the Germans in return for his co-operation and he was assured that his broadcasts would not be censored. Unlike William Joyce, who broadcast blatant Nazi propaganda and referred to England as 'the enemy', Amery was interested in a German victory not for its own sake, but because he believed that it was the only way to defeat Bolshevism, the Jews and America. (Amery's paternal grandmother was a Hungarian Jew; presumably he chose not to mention this in Berlin.)

Amery's presence in Berlin was kept a secret until shortly before the first broadcast, but in November 1942 Leo Amery was finally alerted:

> 17 November – Home to get unpleasant news from an American agency ... that the German wireless has announced that John is in Berlin, apparently staying at the Adlon ... It does look as if the Gestapo had got hold of him and were bent on exploiting him in some way or other.

Leo Amery did not yet know that the German Foreign Office were planning to use Amery's broadcasts to plant the idea in the minds of the British Government that Germany might be prepared to negotiate with Britain. Amery was the son of a British cabinet minister and the Germans believed that this would give his broadcasts a certain weight. It was a terrible mistake. Rebecca West, who reported Amery's trial for the *New Yorker*, put it like this: 'He was known to every newspaper reader in England as the problem child of distinguished parents, who had made countless appearances in police courts, and the sole result of putting him on the air would be to make English listeners feel sympathy with his family and a reiterated conviction that the Germans were terrible cads.'

It was not just the listeners who were sympathetic: on 18 November Churchill gave a speech at Harrow. He drove back to London with Leo Amery, who wrote about their journey in his diary: 'He spoke to me very nicely about my trouble with John. I told him that if the thing in any way embarrassed him from the point of view of his Government I should be only too ready to drop out. "Good God, I wouldn't hear of such a thing!" was his reply, and he said that nobody could blame me for the aberrations of a grown-up son.'

The following day Amery made his first broadcast from Berlin. It was a muddled, anti-Semitic tirade and it concluded with an appeal to his British audience that made him sound almost deranged: 'Between you and peace stands only the Jew and his tool, namely the Bolshevik and American Governments. I am saying that not as a defeatist but as a patriot whose primary concern is the preservation of the British Empire.'

Amery made only seven broadcasts and although they attracted some media attention in Britain to begin with, they made no impact on either the British Government or public opinion. By the end of the year it was clear that his broadcasts had not had the desired effect and he was taken off the air. Rebecca West summed it up: 'Words flowed from Amery's mouth in the conventional groupings of English culture, but he had not intelligence, only a vacancy around which there rolled a snowball of Fascist chatter.' Once the broadcasts were finished, Amery embarked upon the second stage of his self-styled campaign of treason: to set up a British anti-Bolshevik legion to fight against the Russians on the Eastern Front. In April 1943 he went into the internment camp in St Denis in Paris and delivered a speech to a group of prisoners, in the hope of persuading them to join what he referred to as 'St George's Legion'. Predictably, it was a disaster and Amery was unceremoniously shouted down. He returned to Berlin and continued to work for the German Foreign Office, who were still paying all his expenses.

After a brief spell as the news editor on a new 'British' radio station, Amery was sent off on a propaganda tour of occupied Europe. He became engrossed in his fantasy world and finished up in Italy in April 1945. There he met Mussolini and they briefly pooled their delusions before Mussolini was shot and Amery was arrested by the partisans. Rebecca West described what happened next:

> When he was questioned by a British Military Intelligence officer he asked for a typewriter and proceeded to type a statement some thousand words long, which was brilliantly composed, put the noose around his neck, and gave the history of two different people. One of these was a wise young man of lofty principles who sought to reconcile England and Germany in order that together they might fight the rising tide of Communism, and to that end travelled about Europe, a weary Titan urging common sense

> on statesmen who for some reason would not heed the voice of sanity; the other was a crazed harlequin enmeshed in an unfortunate adventure.

In July 1945, two weeks before the general election in which his father lost his seat and the Labour party gained a large majority, Amery was brought to England and taken straight to Bow Street police station, where he was charged with high treason. Two months later, while Amery was on remand in Brixton prison, William Joyce was found guilty of the same offence and sentenced to death.

On 28 November 1945, as Josef Kramer awaited execution in Hameln prison, Amery stood trial at the Old Bailey, charged with eight counts of high treason contrary to the Treason Act of 1351. It was an important trial (Leo Amery and the Conservatives were no longer in government, but he was a well-known public figure) and it was prosecuted by the Attorney General, Sir Hartley Shawcross. Amery was represented by Gerald Slade KC, who had defended William Joyce, and the judge was Mr Justice Humphreys. On the first day of the trial there was a group of Spanish lawyers in court; it had been anticipated that Amery was going to enter a plea of not guilty on the basis that, since he had become a Spanish citizen before the war, he could not technically be a traitor to Britain. The trial was late in starting and when the indictment was put to Amery he pleaded guilty to all counts, contrary to all expectations. Rebecca West was in court: 'A murmur ran through the court which was horrified, which was expostulatory, which was tinged with self-pity, for this was suicide. If he pleaded guilty he must be sentenced to death … In effect, this young man was saying, "I insist on being hanged by the neck in three weeks' time." Very strangely, what he said was felt by the whole court as an act of cruelty. It rejected the life that was in all of us.' Mr Justice Humphreys spoke: 'I never accept a plea of guilty on a capital charge without assuring myself that the accused thoroughly understands what he is doing and what the immediate result must be, and that he is in accord with his legal advisors in the course he has taken.' Amery's barrister was very clear in his answer to the question: 'I can assure you of that, my lord. I have explained the position to my client and I am satisfied he understands it.'

The background was this: in the weeks before the trial Amery's younger brother Julian had gone to Spain to find the evidence to support his defence and returned with a Spanish certificate of naturalisation dated March 1937, but a couple of days before the trial was due to start it had become clear that the certificate was not authentic. This left Amery without a defence, unless he went into the witness box and tried to convince the jury that he had never intended to commit treason. Rebecca West was very disturbed by what had happened: 'It seemed extraordinary that Amery had been allowed to plead guilty. That he had wished to do so was not a satisfactory explanation, for he was too volatile to have resisted whole-hearted pressure, had it been applied.' David Faber's biography of the Amery family makes it clear that Leo and Julian Amery were both party to the discussions with Gerald Slade about whether or not Amery should enter a guilty plea. It was an agonising decision, but in the end they decided that a guilty plea would create a better impression and improve the chances of a reprieve. Amery was consulted about the decision the night before his trial and agreed with their conclusions. Rebecca West thought that Amery had been badly advised:

> Mr Slade hoped that Amery would afterwards be reprieved because he was the son of a loved and valued public servant. The prosecuting counsel … did all he could to dissuade Mr Slade, pointing out that the social climate would never permit such a concession to one of the governing classes, and of course he was right. Mr Slade was in the wrong century … by the time the First World War was over few people in any class would have considered it proper that a great man should be rewarded for his greatness by exemption of his son from the penalty which would certainly have been inflicted on the son of a poor man.

Amery's plea of guilt left the judge with no choice. *The Times* reported that Amery was sentenced to death within eight minutes of entering the dock: 'Amery … took the sentence with complete composure. He bowed to Mr Justice Humphreys when he was brought into court, and also after the sentence had been passed … Amery had kept his eyes on the judge throughout his remarks and while he passed sentence. Showing no sign of emotion, he bowed with dignity to the judge and turned to walk down the steps to the cells.' The Amery family did everything they could to persuade the Home Secretary, James Chuter Ede, to grant a reprieve. Amery's mother, Bryddie, wrote desperately sad letters to Ede, begging him to be merciful to her son, and his father embarked on a campaign to persuade the Home Secretary to grant a reprieve on the basis that, although his son was not insane according to the strict legal definition, he was suffering from a mental disorder. The report of the senior medical officer at Brixton had already concluded that Amery was not suffering from any form of mental illness, but Leo Amery commissioned another psychiatrist. This psychiatrist was not allowed to see Amery, so instead he interviewed a large number of witnesses – former teachers, girlfriends, and so on – who all described Amery's peculiar personality traits. His report concluded that Amery was not technically insane but that he was suffering from a psychopathic disorder which meant that he was 'incapable of a normal appreciation of consequences and [was] devoid of the moral sense by which normal people control their actions and utterances.'

The Home Secretary was now faced with two contradictory reports and he had to respond to pleas for clemency from some very distinguished public figures, including Amery's godfather, who was a former Lord Chancellor, and Amery's headmaster at Harrow, who was now the President of St John's College, Oxford. He took the unusual step of commissioning two more psychiatrists to investigate Amery's case. These psychiatrists concluded that Amery was unable to form moral judgements about his own conduct and that he should not be executed. This left the Home Secretary in a horribly difficult position: clearly Amery *was* suffering from some kind of mental disorder, but he was a traitor and the son of a former cabinet minister. It was a political minefield. He was advised by his Permanent Under-Secretary, Sir Frank Newsam. His advice on the law was that since Amery had not been certified insane, strictly speaking the medical reports were not binding on the Home Secretary. His advice on the politics was exactly as Rebecca West had predicted: 'There is the further consideration of the effect of a reprieve on public opinion. Capital punishment in this country is tolerated as a deterrent because the man in the street believes that the law is administered without fear or favour. If Amery were reprieved it would be difficult to convince the ordinary man that Amery had not received exceptional and privileged treatment.' Leo Amery had failed. At nine o'clock on the morning of 19 December 1945 Pierrepoint entered the condemned cell in Wandsworth prison: 'He was so cool and calm … He said: "I'm pleased to meet you, Mr Pierrepoint, but not under these circumstances."'

In June 1946 Bryddie wrote to the Home Office, asking for permission to put flowers on her son's grave. They refused. In the same year the Corinthian Press in Soho Square, in the centre of London, published a small pamphlet made up of just eleven pages. In the British Library there is a copy of this pamphlet, the pages held together with a thin thread that is no longer white. On the front cover there are four words: 'John Amery. An Explanation'. Below these words are three initials: 'L.S.A.'

> In view of the legal advice that association with the Germans, even if confined to propaganda against the Russians, amounted under the Act of 1351 to adherence to the King's enemies against the Sovereign himself, John felt that he had no possible valid defence in law for conduct for which he did not wish to apologise. He accordingly preferred to plead guilty and to avoid the further distress to his family by uselessly prolonging the proceedings. This has been recognised as a courageous and manly decision. But one of its consequences has been that … there has been no statement of those circumstances … of his case which afford, not indeed a justification, but an intelligible explanation of his sincere conviction that his action

> was in no sense directed against his country, but was inspired by a desire to save the British Empire as well as Europe from a danger which he felt the British Government of the day refused to realise.

Leo Amery wrote the pamphlet and distributed it amongst his friends. It is a father's plea in mitigation for his son, a plea for understanding. It is what every parent wants to say to the teacher when their child has misbehaved: 'Yes, I know he has done wrong. But if you knew him as *I* know him, you would not judge him as you do. Please understand that his motives were not bad. Please love him – he is my child.' Most of the eleven pages are devoted to an explanation of Amery's mistaken belief that he could influence the outcome of the war, and they are largely based on the written submissions that Leo Amery had made to the Home Secretary in his unsuccessful attempt to obtain a reprieve for his son. The final paragraph is a later addition and it includes a poem that Leo Amery wrote for his son just before he visited him for the last time in prison:

> During the long and anxious months of his imprisonment, and, not least, during the last weeks after he had been condemned to death, he maintained an unwavering serenity and even cheerfulness, content to believe that, even if the course of events failed to justify his fears of the Communist peril, he would at any rate be regarded as just one of the casualties of a world revolution in which the accident of his environment, and his own sincere convictions, found him, at the finish, on the wrong side of the barricades.

> In that faith he walked unassisted to his fate, after thanking the prison chaplain and warders for their unfailing courtesy.
>
> At end of wayward days he found a cause
> 'Twas not his Country's' – Only time can tell
> If that defiance of our ancient laws
> Was treason – or foreknowledge. He sleeps well.

So Amery is no longer a traitor but a son to be proud of, a young man with all the virtues closest to the English heart: he is courageous, manly, serene and cheerful. He has even remembered to say thank you. Leo Amery has rescued his son for posterity; he has had the last word – almost.

In the copy of this pamphlet in the British Library, there is a handwritten note underneath the poem. Whoever wrote it must have used a fountain pen and black ink. The handwriting is fluid and seems confident:

> Leo wrote these lines for him. He loved him so and took them with him to his fearless end. His adored father said, 'I am so proud of your courage, you are so brave Jackie.' 'But I am your son', came in a flash, with his lovely smile.

I cannot be sure who wrote these words, but I think I know: I think they were written by Bryddie, John Amery's mother.

CHAPTER SIX

A Man Apart

In July 1945, five months before John Amery was executed, a new Labour government, led by Clement Atlee, came to power with a large majority. Penal reformers were optimistic that the abolition, or at least suspension, of the death penalty would be back on the agenda. In reality penal reform was not a priority for the Government, and it was not until October 1947 that the Home Secretary, James Chuter-Ede, introduced a new Criminal Justice Bill. The bill proposed to abolish some of the more antediluvian sentences that were still on the statute books, including hard labour and whipping, but it was silent on the question of capital punishment.

When the bill was debated in the House of Commons in April 1948, Labour MP Sydney Silverman moved an amendment to suspend capital punishment for five years. Silverman was physically small and intellectually dynamic, a highly respected backbencher whose politics were often to the left of his own party. He had been campaigning for abolition since 1935, and for the next thirty years he was the driving force behind the abolition movement inside Parliament. He was the son of a Liverpudlian draper, and during the First World War he was imprisoned as a conscientious objector. Later he became a lawyer, acting for tenants rather than landlords, workers rather than employers, and he was known for his commitment and integrity. He was a passionate and persuasive advocate, and often spoke without notes. This is how he addressed the House in 1948:

> It is not only the melodrama and sensationalism with which these proceedings are surrounded; it is not only the sordid squalor, every detail of which spreads into newspapers in every one of these crimes … it is not only the relentless finality of this penalty … No one who knows the records can doubt that there have been cases of error, that there have been miscarriages of justice, and that innocent men have in fact been executed … until human judgment is infallible, we have no right to inflict an irrevocable doom. Above all these things, there is the sense which we all have that this penalty, of itself, denies the very principle on which we claim the right to inflict it – namely, the sanctity of human life … the sole justification, if there be one, for the retention of this penalty is that it is necessary to protect society … No one can prove that that is true; no one can prove that it is untrue … but we may compare it and draw inferences from the comparison … with the state of affairs in other countries in which this penalty has been abolished.

Conservative MP Sir David Maxwell Fyfe KC, who had recently led the British legal team at Nuremberg and went on to become Home Secretary in 1951, would not countenance the idea of judicial error: 'Of course, a jury might go wrong, the

Court of Criminal Appeal might go wrong, as might the House of Lords and the Home Secretary: they might all be stricken mad and go wrong. But that is not a possibility which anyone can consider likely. The honourable and learned Member is moving in a realm of fantasy when he makes that suggestion.' The Home Secretary spoke against the amendment and, although there was a free vote, the government front bench abstained. Nevertheless, Silverman's amendment was carried by a large majority and the bill was passed on to the House of Lords. The Lords rejected the amendment by a majority of 153. While Parliament was debating the Criminal Justice Bill, Pierrepoint was looking after his regulars in the Struggler and commuting to Hameln but he didn't have any work from the sheriffs; no executions took place in Britain whilst abolition was on the parliamentary agenda, and they were not resumed until November 1948, after a gap of nine months.

In November Pierrepoint carried out three executions and the Home Secretary announced that the government would set up a Royal Commission on Capital Punishment. Despite the fact that the climate of opinion in the House of Commons was now clearly abolitionist, the Government did not ask the Commission to consider the question of complete abolition. Their terms of reference were to consider whether liability under the law to suffer capital punishment should be limited or modified. On 4 August 1949 Pierrepoint carried out a double execution at Swansea prison and the Royal Commission heard from its first witness. The person who opened the show, the first person to give their evidence to the Royal Commission, was Sir Frank Newsam, KBE, CVO, MC, who was the Permanent Under-Secretary of State at the Home Office.

Sir Frank was a very important man; he was fifty-two when he appeared before the Commission and he had worked in the Home Office for more than twenty years. Educated at St John's College, Oxford, Frank Aubrey Newsam had served honourably in the First World War and taught Classics at Harrow before going into the Civil Service at the age of twenty-seven. It was extremely unusual for such a senior civil servant to remain in the same department for this length of time and it meant that Sir Frank's knowledge and experience of the workings of the Home Office were far superior to that of any of the Home Secretaries he had served. One of Sir Frank's jobs was to advise Home Secretaries on whether to make a recommendation for mercy in capital cases – he had advised Chuter-Ede about the Amery case in 1945 – and his influence was considerable.

At the start of his evidence before the Royal Commission, Sir Frank warmed up with a gentle flex of his mandarin muscles: 'I think it is going to be embarrassing if I am asked for my personal views on any question ... anything I say here in expressing my own opinions might cause him [the Home Secretary] a great deal of trouble afterwards; so that I should like rather to state the arguments for and against any proposal, and though in the course of doing so I may inevitably give a hint as to my own views, I do not want to express them myself.' After this opening Sir Frank gave his evidence with great decorum, keeping his opinions mostly to himself.

For months on end the witnesses trooped in and out of the committee room: bishops, prison governors, prison chaplains, prison officers, policemen, judges, doctors, psychiatrists and prison reformers. On 3 March 1950 the Commission heard evidence from Sir John Anderson, a former Conservative Home Secretary and a trenchant supporter of capital punishment. During the Commons debate two years earlier Sir John had swept aside one of the principal objections to the death penalty, its irrevocability: 'the risk ... of the capital penalty being executed on anyone who was not in fact guilty of the crime of which he had been convicted is so small, indeed infinitesimal, that that consideration can be dismissed.' A week after Sir John gave his evidence to the Royal Commission, Pierrepoint was summoned to Pentonville to execute a young Welshman called Timothy Evans. The execution itself was unremarkable and it was reported very briefly in *The Times*; Sir John probably knew nothing about it.

Although the Commission's main concern was whether there should be an alternative to capital punishment for some types of murder, it had also been asked by the Prime Minister to consider the method of execution. And so Sir Ernest Gowers, the Chairman of the Commission, did something that no one from Whitehall or Westminster had ever done before: he asked to speak to the executioner. In August 1950 Pierrepoint received a letter from 6 Spring Gardens, London SW1: 'The Commission would be glad to have the advantage of hearing evidence from you ... ' It wasn't an invitation that Pierrepoint could refuse, and on 2 November the members of the Commission abandoned their warm committee room in Whitehall for the cold, uncomfortable surroundings of Wandsworth prison, where they watched Pierrepoint carry out a fake execution for their benefit. There were twelve members of the Commission – ten men and two women – and the two women members were not present on 2 November. Pierrepoint was annoyed because the prison officer who had been chosen to act as the condemned prisoner took fright and was reluctant to stand on the trapdoors, making the dummy execution considerably slower than the real thing.

That afternoon Pierrepoint gave his evidence before the Commission. Up to this point in his life Pierrepoint had played his roles with relish and a certain style – the publican with a song and a cigar, the sombre and meticulous professional on the scaffold, the charming and attentive gentleman who looked after the ladies – but being summoned to give evidence before the Royal Commission was not in his script; this was the first time he had come face to face with the Establishment, and he didn't like it. When Pierrepoint was called into the committee room he was asked to sit down next to a female secretary. It was a very bad start – he had made a personal rule that he would never discuss his work as an executioner in the presence of a woman and now he was being asked to do precisely that. He had no choice, but he was not happy about it.

In his autobiography Pierrepoint described how keenly he felt his own lack of education as he faced a barrage of questions from the highly educated people who sat around the table. He felt that his answers would be carefully scrutinised, and he was anxious to maintain his discretion while, at the same time, not saying the wrong thing. He wanted to emerge with his reputation and dignity intact. It wasn't easy: 'Exactly [what] do you do from the moment you arrive at a prison … until the end of the operation? Have you ever … nearly decapitated [the prisoner] or strangled him? … Do you consider that hanging … is as humane and quick as any method of capital punishment could be? … Would you say that there was anything particularly difficult or unpleasant in the execution of a woman?' To begin with his answers were short and stilted. Just as he began to warm up a little, they asked a question that stopped him in his tracks: 'How many executions have you attended as an executioner?' A seemingly benign question which threw him badly. It was an affront to his professional dignity and his natural discretion. He refused to give a figure for publication and he gave the Commission the exact figure later, on the understanding that it would not be made public. The transcript of his evidence gives his answer as being 'some hundreds'. Like Sir Frank Newsam, Pierrepoint had his own professional code of conduct. The Commission was familiar with Sir Frank's code and they respected it, but they appeared to be unaware of Pierrepoint's professional sensibilities.

The Commissioners were curious to know about public opinion:

> *Q:* Have you had any experience of judging what the general opinion of ordinary people in England is about capital punishment? I imagine that people must talk to you about your duties?
> *A:* Yes, but I refuse to speak about it. It is something I think should be secret myself. It is sacred to me really.'

Sacred. It was a surprising word to use, but no one asked Pierrepoint what he meant by it. The Commissioners moved on; they were anxious to know about hangings that had gone wrong:

> *Q:* Have you had any awkward moments?
> *A:* No, I have only seen one in all my career.
> *Q:* What happened?
> *A:* He was rough. It was unfortunate; he was not an Englishman, he was a spy and he kicked up rough.

Pierrepoint did not know it at the time, but the Commissioners had questioned Mr Gedge, the Under-Sheriff for the County of London, about the same incident. This was his reply: 'He was a foreigner, and I personally have noticed that English people take their punishment better than foreigners.' The man they were talking about was Karel Richter, a German spy whom Pierrepoint had hanged in 1941, exactly a year after the executions of Waldberg and Meier in Pentonville.

Richter was dropped by parachute in May 1941, arrested within a couple of days and sentenced to death in October of the same year. He was a tall, heavily built man who weighed fifteen stone and four pounds. Pierrepoint entered Richter's cell just before nine o'clock on the morning of 10 December 1941 and found Richter waiting for him in the opposite corner of the cell. When he saw Pierrepoint he turned and deliberately ran into the wall, smacking his head hard against the stone and falling to the ground. Five prison officers restrained him as he tried to raise himself up again, and in this scrum Pierrepoint strapped Richter's arms behind his back. Then, as usual, Pierrepoint led the way to the scaffold.

In his desperation Richter continued to fight. He twisted and writhed and did what no one had ever done before: ripped the strap. One eyelet tore and he broke free. (Pierrepoint never replaced the torn strap, he simply fastened it on a different eyelet. It was this strap that he kept in the suitcase under the bed in Southport, the one that he had tried out on Tommy Mann.)

After a ghastly struggle the warders held Richter down on the floor while Pierrepoint, throwing caution and courtesy to the winds, shoved his knee into the small of Richter's back and pulled the strap tightly so that it could fasten on the next eyelet. Richter never stopped fighting; he was wrestled onto the scaffold and leapt off the trap. The jump caused the noose to slip and for a moment Pierrepoint thought that the noose would slip over Richter's head. In fact the rope caught between his upper lip and his nose and his spinal cord broke in exactly the right place.

Koestler used the Richter extract from the Royal Commission's Report in his abolitionist polemic, *Reflections on Hanging*, to illustrate the peculiarities of the British tradition of hanging: 'There you are. Hanging is quite all right for Englishmen; they actually seem to like it; it is only the foreigners who cause trouble. The outsider appreciates neither the clean fun, nor the solemn ritualistic aspect of the procedure, nor the venerable tradition behind it.'

Unlike Pierrepoint, Sir Frank was quite at home in the committee room of the Royal Commission and he used his professional neutrality to great effect. He was anxious that the Commission should consider whether the public's perception of capital punishment was influenced by the method of execution: 'I feel (I have no evidence about it) that a large amount of repugnance to capital punishment is due to the horror that certain sensitive people feel about the degradation of the human frame by stringing it up.' These were strong words for a civil servant. He returned to the issue twice: 'I personally would not express an opinion, but I would like the question considered … I am still not happy about this. The Home Office would like you to take evidence on this question and advise whether one of the objections to capital punishment is not the degradation of the human body by stringing it up by the neck.' Reading the transcript, it is hard to resist the inference that Sir Frank did, indeed, have a personal opinion about hanging, and that it was not one that Pierrepoint would have agreed with.

The Commission was sitting in private on the afternoon of

2 November, but Pierrepoint knew that his evidence would be published. When he had finished he came out into Trafalgar Square. He felt himself transformed by the experience: 'This morning you belonged to a remote and skilled mystery. Now you are at one with this crowd.' He decided that although he could now sell his story with impunity, he would forbear. His description of this moment in his autobiography is typically self-serving: 'As long as I was connected to this craft, I should continue as a man apart.' He was connected to the craft for another six years. During that time a great deal was written about him, but he continued, in his own mind at least, as a man apart. He had been stripped of his mystery, but he kept faith.

CHAPTER SEVEN

Derek Bentley

On 28 January 1953, two years after he had given evidence to the Royal Commission, Pierrepoint hanged Derek Bentley. By this time the Pierrepoints had moved on to a much bigger pub, the Rose and Crown in Hoole, near Preston. According to Tommy Mann, it made Pierrepoint a fortune. Coachloads of men would stop by on their way back to Liverpool after a day out in Blackpool because they wanted to see the executioner. Generally they would get home late, after a few drinks, so they needed a peace offering to take back with them. Pierrepoint built a greenhouse at the back of the pub and Anne started selling flowers for the trippers' wives. 'They were very good at business.' In 1953 the trippers came in droves to the Rose and Crown – it was a year of controversial executions, and more controversy meant more beer was sold.

The execution of Derek Bentley was particularly shocking: Bentley was a nineteen-year-old epileptic, with an IQ of 77 (at the time this indicated 'borderline feeble minded') and the reading age of a four-year-old. In the view of a child psychologist who examined him in 1949 he was 'of borderline subnormal intelligence' and 'educationally very retarded'. He was the third child in a family of five and his childhood had been dominated by the war. During the Blitz, when the family were living in Blackfriars, Bentley's sister, aunt and grandmother were all killed in a bombing raid, and when he was eleven the family's flat was hit by a flying bomb.

The Bentley family moved four times in the first twelve years of Bentley's life and his education was hopelessly disrupted; when he started secondary school he could not read or write properly, he was suffering from severe headaches, he was bullied, and then he truanted. By the time he was fifteen Bentley had been in front of the magistrates twice, for shop breaking and theft, and he was sent to an approved school in Bristol for two years. There he was labelled 'educationally subnormal', but nobody seemed able to help him. He was released in 1950 and returned to the family home in Croydon where he spent a year doing very little and rarely leaving the house – his headaches worsened and he began taking the barbiturate phenobarbitone.

During the summer of 1952 Bentley started to go around with a sixteen-year-old called Christopher Craig. They had been at the same school for some time, although they had not been friends before 1952. Craig was a troubled boy from an educated, middle-class background, and Bentley's parents believed that he was an evil boy who led their son astray. Craig was the youngest of nine children and his siblings were all leading unremarkable lives, with the exception of his older brother, Niven. In September 1952, shortly after Craig began to spend time with Bentley, Niven was charged with armed robbery. At the end of October he was sentenced to twelve years' imprisonment. Three days later Craig and Bentley were arrested and charged with murder.

The facts of the case, as they emerged at the trial, are these: on the evening of 2 November Craig and Bentley climbed onto the flat roof of a warehouse in Croydon with the intention of breaking into it. They were seen by Mrs Ware who lived in a house opposite, and the police were called. Detective Constable Fairfax was the first officer to arrive and when he got up onto the roof he grabbed hold of Bentley. After DC Fairfax had taken hold of Bentley, Craig shot and injured Fairfax. The police witnesses at the trial gave evidence that just before Craig fired the gun Bentley had shouted to him, 'Let him have it, Chris,' but Bentley denied this. Fairfax searched Bentley and found a knuckleduster and a knife. More police officers arrived and Craig fired at them. Police Constable Sydney Miles, who had two young children at home and twenty-two years of service in the police behind him, was shot between the eyes and died instantly. One of the other police officers gave evidence that Craig shouted out, 'I am Craig. You have just given my brother twelve years. Come on, you coppers. I'm only sixteen.'

Bentley was taken off the roof and as he reached the top of the stairwell he shouted out, 'They're taking me down, Chris.' DC Fairfax then returned to the roof with a firearm that had been issued to him. After Craig had fired several more shots and Fairfax had fired twice, Craig jumped off the roof and crashed down into a greenhouse. He broke several bones but he did not lose consciousness, and the first police officer who got to him reported Craig as saying, 'I wish I were fucking dead. I hope I have killed the fucking lot.' Craig and Bentley were arrested and charged with the murder of PC Miles. Later that night the police searched Craig's house and found a bullet, the sawn-off barrel of his gun and a quantity of ammunition in a tin box. Bentley was interviewed at Croydon police station at four o'clock in the morning: 'I didn't kill him, guv. Craig did it.'

On 9 December 1952 Craig and Bentley stood trial at the Old Bailey. London was immersed in a profound sulphur dioxide smog, but this didn't deter the crowds who queued outside the Old Bailey. The killing of a police officer in the course of his duty was a rare and truly shocking event in 1952 and there was huge public sympathy for PC Miles's family. A year later Reginald Paget, a Labour MP and a QC, wrote a powerful piece of campaigning literature about the Craig and Bentley case, arguing that it was a miscarriage of justice. This is what he said about the killing of PC Miles:

> To Englishmen the killing of a policeman is perhaps the most serious of all crimes, and we are right so to regard it, for of all civilised people we in Britain have the least cause to fear our police. It is more than a symbol that our police go unarmed – it is a condition of our liberty and when men take advantage of our unarmed police they are threatening the whole of our liberties.

In 1952 there was also an increasing fearfulness about the rise in violent crime, a fear created in part by lurid newspaper reports of juvenile delinquency. Despite the fact that both boys came from respectable families, they became a focus for the moral outrage of the popular press: 'You can't leave it to the schools, the churches, the BBC, or the youth clubs. You can't pass the buck to the Welfare State, or the police … At the heart of the problem of teenage gangsters … lies this inescapable fact: too many parents do not take enough trouble with their children.'

In 1950 Ealing Studios had released *The Blue Lamp*, starring Jack Warner as a heroic working-class copper. The film, which was a huge success, both critically and commercially, was dedicated to the police service and had the full approval and co-operation of the Metropolitan Police. The hero – PC George Dixon – is an idealised bobby, a decent and dependable bloke who goes home to tend to his begonias and treats his wife ('Ma') with the respect she deserves. George has been on the beat for twenty-five years and he is a pillar of the community; he helps old ladies cross the road, tolerates the drunks with a twinkle in his eye and moves on the street traders with a friendly nod. Back at the station he sings in the police male voice choir and mucks in with the boys.

The film tells the story of what happens when George Dixon comes up against a new kind of criminal: the juvenile delinquent. The serious voiceover leaves the audience in no doubt about the enemy: 'A type of delinquent responsible for the post-war increase in crime … Youths with brain enough to organise criminal adventures and yet they lack the necessary experience of the professional thief.' The film is kind to the latter, the pre-war criminal who knows his business and plays by the rules. The old-style criminal and the old-style copper have a mutual understanding, even a mutual respect. The juvenile delinquent, Riley (played by Dirk Bogarde), is a loose canon: he doesn't know what the rules are, and even if he did, he wouldn't play by them. Riley is mad, bad and dangerous to know. He wears sharp suits, great hats, and is very sexy. In contrast to the police, who act for the communal good, Riley is only interested in personal gain.

Riley lives with a hapless young innocent who has been seduced by him into a world of violent crime. The sex and the violence are intimately linked – Riley embraces his girl and caresses his gun with equal fervour. Finally Riley shoots Dixon in the course of a robbery and Dixon dies. The hunt is on – Riley is an elusive prey, but slowly the police close in. Riley gets more dangerous and even sexier (Dirk Bogarde in a tight but ragged jumper). In the final scene Riley is pursued into the White City Stadium and the police hunt him down amidst the dog-racing crowds. The analogy is not subtle: the dogs are after the hare. All the old lags are at the races, and a detective in a raincoat asks for their help: 'He shot that copper.' 'I see. That's different.' Riley has transgressed and the old order must prevail. In the end he is trapped in the tunnels under the stadium, surrounded on one side by the police and on the other by the criminals who know that shooting a copper is wrong. (PC Dixon was resurrected in 1955 and appeared in 434 episodes of *Dixon of Dock Green*, which ran continuously until 1976 and at its peak attracted audiences of 14 million.)

At the trial of Derek Bentley and Christopher Craig the judge was Lord Chief Justice Goddard, a well-known advocate of the death penalty, who had said in his evidence to the Royal Commission that too many reprieves were granted to people who had been sentenced to death. Christmas Humphreys, the son of Mr Justice Humphreys – who had tried John Amery, opened the case for the prosecution: this was a joint enterprise, he said, during the course of which Craig had deliberately and wilfully murdered PC Miles. Bentley had 'incited Craig to begin the shooting and, although technically under arrest at the actual time of the killing of Miles, was party to that murder and equally responsible in law.' The words 'Let him have it, Chris' were said to be a deliberate incitement to murder, spoken to a man whom Bentley clearly knew had a gun. The words 'They're taking me down, Chris' were a further incitement to Craig to shoot at the police. The prosecution alleged that on the way to the police station Bentley had said, 'I knew he had a gun but I didn't think he'd use it', and that when he had made a statement under caution at the police station he had said, 'I did not know he was going to use the gun.'

Craig's defence was that he was guilty of manslaughter, not murder, because he had only intended to frighten the police officers, not to kill them. Francis Cassels represented Bentley; his defence was that he had never entered into any kind of agreement with Craig that a gun would be used and that he had never incited Craig to fire it. He didn't know that Craig had a gun until he fired the first shot, and he never said, 'Let him have it, Chris.' He said that when he shouted, 'They're taking me down, Chris', his intention was to warn Craig not to shoot in his direction. He denied both the admissions about the gun, and it was suggested by his counsel that the words in the statement came about as a result of a question that was put to him by the police – 'Did you know that he was going to use the gun?'

Cassels had to tread a very fine line; he didn't want to allege explicitly that the police officers were lying, so instead he chose to emphasise the discrepancies in the police evidence, suggesting that they were mistaken or confused about what they had heard and seen and therefore the jury could not rely on their evidence. It must have been a difficult call: for weeks the newspapers had been full of the tragedy of PC Miles and the crisis of juvenile delinquency that was engulfing post-war Britain, and allegations of police corruption were extremely rare and treated with enormous suspicion. To claim that three police officers were deliberately lying to the court would have been an act of rebellion – it might pay off but it was more likely that it would turn the jury against his client. Cassels also had to consider the possibility that a direct attack on the police could allow the prosecution to introduce evidence of Bentley's criminal record and, if he was convicted, it might subsequently reduce his chances of being granted a reprieve. On the other hand, if Cassels did *not* directly attack the credibility of the police, he would be cross-examining them with one hand tied behind his back and there was a real danger that the defence would look weak. He chose decorum over rebellion, but nevertheless it was a difficult trial, dominated by the presence of the Lord Chief Justice.

Goddard interrupted throughout the trial, usually to draw attention to a point that supported the case for the prosecution and emphasised the weaknesses in the defence case. When he came to sum up the case to the jury, this is what he said about the gun issue:

> The first thing you have to consider is: Did Bentley know that Craig was armed? Now, you know, because I sit on the bench and you sit in the jury-box it is not necessary that we leave our common-sense at home. The great virtue of trial by jury is that jurymen can exercise the common-sense of ordinary people. Can you suppose for a moment, especially when you have heard Craig say that why he carried a revolver was for the purpose of boasting and making himself a big man, that he would not have told his pals he was out with that he had got a revolver? Is it not almost inconceivable that Craig would not have told him, and probably shown him, the revolver which he had? That is quite apart from what Bentley said afterwards. I should think you would come to the conclusion that the first thing, almost, Craig would tell him, if they

> were going on a shop-breaking expedition, was: 'It's all right. I've got a revolver with me.'

Goddard then dealt with the question of whether Bentley had shouted out to Craig to incite him to shoot:

> There is one thing I am sure I can say with the assent of all you twelve gentlemen, that the police officers that night, and those three officers in particular [Fairfax, McDonald and Harrison], showed the highest gallantry and resolution; they were conspicuously brave. Are you going to say they are conspicuous liars? Because if their evidence is untrue that Bentley called out 'Let him have it, Chris!', those three officers are doing their best to swear away the life of that boy. If it is true, it is, of course, the most deadly piece of evidence against him. Do you believe that those three officers have come into the box and sworn what is deliberately untrue – those three officers who on that night showed a devotion to duty for which they are entitled to the thanks of the community?

It was an extraordinarily biased summing-up. Lord Chief Justice Goddard ignored completely one of the most fundamental rules of a jury trial, that the judge must be impartial and balanced at all times, and he decided to deliver a summing-up for the prosecution. The jury took seventy-eight minutes to find both defendants guilty of murder. In the case of Bentley they made a recommendation for mercy. (Whenever a jury made a recommendation for mercy, they did so entirely on their own initiative; judges were not allowed to prompt them, or even to remind them of the power.

The recommendation was not binding on the Home Secretary, although he had to take it into account. It was always open to a trial judge to support a jury's recommendation and express his support to the Home Secretary, in private. If that happened it was very probable, although not certain, that a reprieve would be granted. On the other hand, the Home Secretary was perfectly entitled to ignore a jury's recommendation, and regularly did so.) Craig was under eighteen, so there was only one sentence available to the judge: he was detained during Her Majesty's pleasure. Bentley was nineteen, so again there was only one sentence available to the judge: he was sentenced to death. Pierrepoint was waiting.

On 13 January 1953 the Court of Appeal heard Bentley's appeal. There were two main grounds: firstly, that in his summing-up the judge had not given an adequate description of Bentley's defence, instead summarising it in two brief sentences, and secondly that he had failed to direct the jury on the issue of whether Bentley had withdrawn from the joint enterprise at the point when he was arrested by Fairfax on the rooftop, before PC Miles was shot. Bizarrely, Francis Cassels did not consider it worth mentioning in the appeal that Lord Chief Justice Goddard had given a summing-up so grossly prejudicial in its entirety that it had deprived him of a fair trial. The appeal was dismissed and the execution date was set for 28 January, but there was still a strong belief that Bentley would be granted a reprieve. There was so much in his favour: his age, his mental age, the fact that he did not pull the trigger or even have a gun, the jury's recommendation for mercy and, of course, the fact that Craig, the more guilty of the two, was not going to hang. If Bentley did not qualify for a reprieve, who would?

There were no statutes or written rules to guide the Home

Secretary in the exercise of mercy, just the wisdom of senior civil servants like Sir Frank Newsam and the decisions made by Home Secretaries before him. By 1953 it was a well-established practice for the Home Secretary to review every capital case to see if there were grounds for a reprieve, whether or not there had been a recommendation for mercy from the jury, or an appeal for clemency from the condemned person. When the Home Secretary decided to grant a reprieve he would, technically, advise the Crown to exercise the Royal Prerogative of Mercy and the sentence would be commuted to life imprisonment.

The exercise of the Royal Prerogative was the only way to mitigate the effects of the mandatory death sentence, and the frequent use of the Prerogative became, in itself, a damning criticism of the rigidity of the law; in the first half of the twentieth century, 45 per cent of the people sentenced to death in England and Wales were granted a reprieve. This is a startling figure, not least because it reveals the extent to which the decision about who would live and who would die had become a political, rather than a judicial, decision. It was a political decision that was not open to any form of scrutiny: the grounds on which the decision was based were never disclosed and there was no appeal. The discretion of the Home Secretary was unfettered. MPs were allowed to challenge the decision in the House of Commons, but they had to wait until after the execution.

In 1953 the Report of the Royal Commission on Capital Punishment, whose members had heard evidence from the Home Office, noted that 'a certain broad-based body of doctrine seems to have grown up in the Home Office, whose representatives were good enough to give us some indication of the practice followed by successive Home Secretaries.' So, gently and softly, almost discreetly, the veil was lifted, just a little.

Nothing unexpected was revealed; in very limited types of cases a reprieve would be almost a foregone conclusion: so-called mercy killings, the survivors of genuine suicide pacts and mothers who had killed their children. There was a much longer list of the types of cases which required 'specially close scrutiny', including unpremeditated murders committed in 'some sudden excess of frenzy, where the murderer has previously had no evil animus towards his victim, especially if he is weak-minded or emotionally unstable to an abnormal degree' and murders committed by two or more people with differing degrees of responsibility. In addition, there was the question of age: 'youth, though not in itself a sufficient ground for reprieve in a heinous case, is always taken into account with other mitigating circumstances.' Lastly, there were those 'rare classes of case in which reprieves may be granted'. These included cases where the Home Secretary felt that there was a 'scintilla of doubt about the guilt of the condemned man', and cases where a reprieve had been granted 'in deference to a widely spread or strong local expression of public opinion, on the ground that it would do more harm than good to carry out the sentence if the result was to arouse sympathy for the offender and hostility to the law.' (This is early spin: better lose the spectacle than lose control of its meaning.) The report concluded that the system 'works well in the sense that it produces results generally regarded as broadly satisfactory'.

Bentley's lawyers and his family launched a public campaign and there was tremendous popular support for their case: 14,000 people signed a petition to the Home Secretary calling on him to grant a reprieve and hundreds of telegrams were sent to the Home Office. On 23 January, when Bentley's father and his sister delivered the petition, Mr Bentley senior made a statement to the press on the steps of the Home Office: 'Remember, a boy's life is in the balance. No amount of legal arguments or books written afterwards will bring him back to life. We, his family, feel sure that we can leave the fair-minded British public to make up their minds and to take every action within their rights to save my son.'

The Home Secretary was Sir David Maxwell Fyfe KC, who had dismissed with such disdain the possibility of judicial error when it was raised during the 1948 parliamentary debate on abolition. Maxwell Fyfe did not seem to care for the views of the British public, fair-minded or otherwise, nor for the opinion of his Permanent Under-Secretary, Sir Frank Newsam, who advised that there should be a reprieve. On 24 January the Bentley family received a letter from the Home Office, informing them that the Home Secretary 'has failed to discover any sufficient ground to justify him in advising Her Majesty to interfere with the due course of the law'. In his memoirs Maxwell Fyfe described his decision as a 'sombre responsibility', and he reminded his readers of one particular aspect of the Bentley case that he had to consider: 'the possible effects of my decision upon the police force, by whom the murder of a police officer is justly regarded as the most heinous of crimes … It is a bleak, solitary, miserable position for any sensitive or imaginative man, and I am sure that most Home Secretaries have approached their decision as I did, with an overwhelming anxiety to find any factors which would justify a recommendation for mercy.'

In the House of Commons Maxwell Fyfe's decision had enraged a large number of MPs and the day before the execution Sydney Silverman tried to force a debate on the Bentley case. In the words of Reginald Paget: 'A three-quarter witted boy of nineteen is to be hung for a murder he did not commit and which was committed fifteen minutes after he was arrested. Can we be made to keep silent when a thing as horrible and shocking as that is happening?' The answer was yes, and the debate was not allowed.

On the afternoon of 27 January, on his way to Wandsworth prison, Pierrepoint stopped off at Scotland Yard to have a cup of tea with his old friend Detective Superintendent Daws. Hearing that the prison was surrounded by angry crowds, Daws asked Pierrepoint if he had a Home Office escort to get him into Wandsworth. He had not. Daws promptly arranged for a police car to take his friend into the prison. At ten o'clock on the evening of 27 January the Home Secretary announced that he would not alter his decision; later still, a deputation of six MPs, headed by Aneurin Bevan, and including a former Solicitor General, went to see the Home Secretary, taking with them a motion that had been signed by 200 MPs. At the same time an angry group of protestors marched from the Houses of Parliament to the Home Office and then on to the Home Secretary's house. Sir David was immovable: Pierrepoint's journey would not be wasted.

At nine o'clock the following morning Pierrepoint hanged Derek Bentley. More than 500 people waited outside Wandsworth prison; afterwards, when a prison officer opened the gates to put up the notice of execution, the crowd pressed forward and the notice, which had been placed behind a glass frame, was smashed. (Later the same day a Mr John Rees, of Battersea Park Road, was charged with wilfully damaging a pane of glass worth £1. He pleaded guilty and was fined 20 shillings and ordered to pay 20 shillings in costs.) In the same year that Bentley was hanged, DC Fairfax, who had been shot in the shoulder by Christopher Craig, was awarded the George Cross.

A year later Sir David Maxwell Fyfe, now Viscount Kilmuir, became Lord Chancellor. In 1963 Christopher Craig was released from prison. In 1993, forty years after the execution, it was officially acknowledged that Bentley should never have been hanged and he was granted a limited posthumous pardon. This pardon did not overturn the conviction and in 1998 the Court of Appeal heard a second appeal, conducted on Bentley's behalf by his niece. This is what Lord Chief Justice Bingham said about Lord Chief Justice Goddard's summing-up: 'The language used was not that of a judge but of an advocate … In our judgement the summing- up in this case was such as to deny the appellant that fair trial which is the birthright of every British citizen.' This time, the appeal was allowed.

CHAPTER EIGHT

Evans and Christie

In March 1953, two months after the execution of Derek Bentley, the bodies of four women were discovered in a shabby, cramped house in west London. This discovery eventually led to two terrible revelations: firstly, that a man called John Christie had killed at least seven women in the preceding ten years, and secondly, that a man called Timothy Evans, who had lived in the same house as Christie, had been wrongly accused of murder. Christie was convicted of murder, and Pierrepoint hanged him at Pentonville on 15 July 1953, but that did not help Timothy Evans – Pierrepoint had hanged him three years earlier, also at Pentonville.

The real story behind the Timothy Evans case emerged in the 1960s, largely due to Ludovic Kennedy's book *Ten Rillington Place*. All the subsequent accounts of the case, including this one, are hugely indebted to that book. Timothy Evans was born in 1924 in a small Welsh mining village. His father left his mother while she was pregnant with Evans and he never met him. When Evans was eleven the family moved to London because his stepfather, who had lost his job in the mines as a result of the Depression, had found work as a painter and decorator. Although Evans returned briefly to stay with relatives in Wales, he spent most of his teenage years in west London. He always struggled at school and his learning difficulties were aggravated by frequent and prolonged absences from school as a result of a cut on his foot which became septic and caused serious medical problems throughout his childhood; by the time he was sixteen his foot was permanently deformed, he walked with a slight limp and he was unable to read or write.

In 1949 Evans had the mental age of a ten-year-old and the vocabulary of a fourteen-year-old. His mother said that he was constantly boasting and lying to make himself feel better, to cover up his sense of inadequacy. In 1947, when he was twenty-three years old, Evans married Beryl, who was eighteen. To begin with they lived at home with Evans's mother, step-father and two sisters. In 1948 Beryl became pregnant and it was clear that one bedroom would no longer do; when Beryl was three months pregnant they moved into a tiny top-floor flat at 10 Rillington Place.

The Evans's daughter, Geraldine, was born in October 1948; Beryl stayed at home to look after the baby and Evans worked long hours as a driver for a food company. At this point the relationship between Evans and Beryl was sporadically stormy; Evans was unfaithful and there is evidence that they fought in a predictable way: they were very young, very hard-up, always in debt, and they were living in two small rooms with a young baby. Before Geraldine's first birthday Beryl discovered that she was pregnant again; she was adamant that she did not want another child and, against Evans's wishes, she took pills to try to induce a miscarriage. The pills didn't work and by the beginning of November 1949 Beryl was desperate to have an abortion but unsure what to do about it. She was a respectable girl – finding out where to go for an illegal abortion was difficult and she couldn't afford to do it legally.

At that time abortion was not legal, except on limited medical grounds. Beryl would not have qualified for a 'therapeutic termination' and, unlike thousands of middle-class women, she could not afford to pay a doctor to say that she did qualify. Backstreet abortions were a gamble, and Beryl needed advice because they were performed by a variety of different people with quite different motives: responsible, qualified doctors who were prepared to break the law out of sympathy for the women they treated; middle-aged women who usually intervened with a syringe in the early weeks of pregnancy and acted out of empathy or avarice or a combination of the two; and professional abortionists who often pretended to be doctors but were in reality unqualified and unscrupulous profiteers. Hundreds of women were dying every year after undergoing dangerous backstreet abortions, and the newspapers regularly reported cases of abortionists who had been convicted and sentenced to long terms of imprisonment.

On 30 November 1949 Evans walked into Merthyr Tydfil police station and told the officer on duty that he wanted to give himself up: 'I have disposed of my wife.' Evans then made a number of confused and contradictory statements. To begin with he said that his wife had died after taking a drug to induce a miscarriage and that he had put her body down the drain. The police investigated and found no body. When they suggested to Evans that his wife's body had never been in the drain Evans gave them another account: 'No. I said that to protect a man named Christie … I'll tell you the truth now.' This time he alleged that his wife had died after the man who lived on the ground floor, a Mr John Christie, had attempted to perform an abortion on her. According to Evans, Christie had told him that he had some medical knowledge because he had started to train as a doctor before the war, and although Evans did not want his wife to have an abortion he knew that she had asked Christie to do it while Evans was out at work. When he came home from work Christie had told him that the abortion had gone wrong and that as a consequence his wife had died. He told Evans that his wife's stomach was 'septic poisoned'. His wife's body was on their bed, covered with the eiderdown, and when Evans pulled the eiderdown back he saw that she had been bleeding from the mouth and nose and 'the bottom part'.

Evans told the police that Christie had said that he was going to dispose of the body to avoid getting into trouble with the police and that he would put it down a drain. Meanwhile Christie had taken his wife's body and left it in the first-floor flat because the man who lived there was in hospital at the time. Christie had also told him that he would make arrangements for the Evans's baby to be looked after by a family in Acton and he had rejected Evans's suggestion that he should take the baby to his mother's house, because he said that would arouse suspicions. The following night Christie had told Evans to pack some clothes for the baby because the couple from Acton would be collecting her the following day. When he returned from work the following evening the baby had gone. Shortly afterwards, at Christie's suggestion, he sold his furniture and left London. At this point the police were treating everything that Evans told them with some caution, suspecting that they might be dealing with a hopeless fantasist whose wife had left him, not a vicious killer. The following day they interviewed the man who lived in the ground-floor flat at 10 Rillington Place.

John Reginald Halliday Christie was fifty-one years old and he came from a large, comfortable, middle-class family in Halifax. He had been a scholarship boy, active in the Scouts and a member of the church choir. During the First World War he joined the Army and served behind the lines with the Duke of Wellington's Regiment. He was knocked unconscious by a mustard-gas shell and treated in a military hospital in Calais. After the war Christie returned to Halifax, worked as a clerk in a wool mill and married a local girl called Ethel. He left Ethel after four years and moved to London, leaving behind the disapproval of his family and three criminal convictions: two for dishonesty and one for violence.

In London he was hit by a car and, after he had recovered from his injuries, he began a life characterised by occasional petty crime, sporadic employment and relationships with prostitutes. In 1929 he was sentenced to six months' hard labour for a serious attack on a prostitute with whom he was living and in 1933 he served three months' imprisonment for theft. During this sentence he wrote to Ethel, asking her to live with him again. She agreed and they found a flat in west London.

At this point Christie stopped committing low-level offences and the official records that exist for these years are mainly doctor's notes – he was constantly visiting his GP complaining of bad nerves, headaches, insomnia, stomach pains and so on. In 1938, when Christie was nearly forty years old, he and his wife moved into the ground-floor flat at 10 Rillington Place. A year later he joined the War Reserve Police as a Special Constable. (The police had failed to check whether he had a criminal record.) He was attached to Harrow Road police station and he worked hard – a dedicated officer of the law, committed to the job, battling on amidst the chaos of the Blitz and the deprivations of wartime London. He trained in first aid and he received two commendations for the successful prosecution of criminals.

Towards the end of 1944, for no apparent reason, Christie left the police force. Four years later, in 1948, Timothy and Beryl Evans moved into the top-floor flat at 10 Rillington Place. To them, and to everyone else in Rillington Place, the Christies appeared to be a thoroughly respectable couple.

When Christie was interviewed by the police at the end of November 1950, he denied all the allegations that Evans had made against him and he gave them an account of Evans that included several potentially incriminating details. He described Evans as 'a bit mental' and he told the police that Evans had a history of violence towards his wife: 'Mrs Evans has told my wife and I on more than one occasion that he has assaulted her and grabbed hold of her throat. She said that he had a violent temper and one time would do her in.' He said that both he and his wife had known of Mrs Evans's pregnancy and had tried to dissuade her from taking any tablets; they had not seen Mrs Evans or the baby for about three weeks. The police were impressed by his record of service and by his quiet, calm demeanour. They had no reason to suspect him, apart from the curious, half-baked, contradictory allegations that Evans had made. They searched the house but didn't notice anything suspicious.

By 2 December the police still had no news of the whereabouts of Mrs Evans and her daughter and they were becoming more concerned. They searched the house again and for the first time they also searched the wash house at the bottom of the garden. There they found the bodies of Mrs Evans and her daughter. The Home Office pathologist examined them and concluded that they had been dead for about three weeks and that in both cases death had been caused by asphyxiation due to strangulation. He found that Beryl's right eye and upper lip were badly swollen and that she had bruising inside her vagina, but he did not take a swab from the vagina. Beryl was sixteen weeks pregnant and there was no evidence that any attempt had been made to interfere with the pregnancy. Evans was escorted from Merthyr Tydfil to London and deliberately kept in ignorance of the reason for the journey.

When Evans arrived at Notting Hill police station he was immediately shown the clothes that his wife and daughter had been wearing when they were killed, the cloth and cord that his wife's body had been wrapped in and the tie that had been used to strangle his baby. As Evans stared at these objects, not understanding what it was that he was looking at, Chief Inspector Jennings told him that the bodies of his wife and baby had been found that morning in the wash house at 10 Rillington Place, concealed behind some timber, and that the cause of death in both cases was strangulation. Jennings then said this: 'I have reason to believe that you were responsible for their deaths.'

According to the evidence given by the police at Evans's trial, when Inspector Jennings stopped speaking, Evans spoke just one word in response: 'Yes.' He then proceeded to confess to the murder of his wife and child. In this confession he described how his wife had got into debt, how she nagged him, how they had fought and argued for days, culminating in a fight on 8 November when he hit her across the face with his hand and she hit him back. 'In a fit of temper I grabbed a piece of rope from a chair which I had brought home off my van and strangled her with it.' He went on to say that later that night he had wrapped his wife's body in the cloth that had been shown to him earlier and put the body in the wash house, hiding it behind pieces of wood. He told police that two days later, on 10 November, he had gone to work as usual, and then returned to 10 Rillington Place: 'I then went home, picked up my baby from the cot in the bedroom, picked up my tie and strangled her with it.' Then he described putting the baby's body in the wash house later that night.

Evans was charged with the murder of his wife and child, although when he stood trial he faced an indictment containing just one count: in 1949 a defendant in a murder trial could only be tried on one count of murder, even if the evidence disclosed more than one murder, and in this case the prosecution decided that Evans should be tried for the murder of his baby (partly because he had confessed that the murder of his wife had taken place during a fight and they wanted to avoid the possibility that Evans would rely on a defence of provocation to reduce the verdict to manslaughter, and partly because the murder of the baby occurred after the murder of the wife and this allowed the prosecution to introduce evidence of the earlier murder at the trial).

Within two weeks Evans had retracted his confession and returned to the second story that he had told the police in Wales, that Christie had convinced him that his wife had died as a result of a botched abortion. Before Evans made his confession at Notting Hill police station he had heard (and seen) the details of the murder, and it is very likely that the police officers, whilst acting in good faith, were over-zealous: believing absolutely in Evans's guilt, their anxiety to secure a conviction may have led them to put pressure on Evans to give the answers they wanted. The real problem was that neither Evans, nor anyone else involved in the case, could think of any reason why Christie might have murdered his upstairs neighbour and her young baby, whereas the prosecution could suggest a number of reasons why Evans might have murdered his wife, most of them contained in Evans's confession.

On 11 January 1950 Evans stood trial at the Old Bailey. The prosecution, conducted by Christmas Humphreys, relied principally upon Evans's confession and Christie's evidence. Christie gave evidence that he had last seen Beryl and the baby on 8 November and that in the middle of the night of 8 November he had heard a loud thud coming from upstairs at 10 Rillington Place: 'As though something was being moved, something heavy was being moved.' After that Evans had told him that Beryl had gone to Bristol, taking the baby with her. It was put to Christie that he had been responsible for both deaths. He denied every allegation that was put to him, politely but firmly. All the contemporary observers agreed that he was a very convincing witness; injured in a gas attack in the First World War, a Special Constable in the Second World War, articulate but softly spoken, suffering from ill health – he was unassailable. Even the evidence of his previous convictions did not seem to carry much weight – the last one was seventeen years earlier and since then he had lived a spotless life. His evidence was corroborated by his wife (nobody has ever really established what Mrs Christie did or did not know about the Evans case).

The defence only called one witness: Timothy Evans. His evidence was essentially the same as his second account to the police in Wales, and he said that he had made a false confession for two reasons – firstly because he was so shocked at hearing of the death of his child that he did not care what happened to him, and secondly because he was frightened and he thought that if he did not tell the police what they wanted to hear they would take him downstairs and start knocking him about. He was expertly cross-examined by Christmas Humphreys and he got into a terrible muddle. There is no doubt that during his dealings with the police Evans had told a lot of lies and the cross-examination uncovered all of them. He sounded confused and unreliable. These were the last three questions of the cross-examination:

> *Q:* Now, you are the person who alleges that Mr Christie is the murderer in this case; can you suggest why he should have strangled your wife?
> *A:* Well, he was at home all day.
> *Q:* Can you suggest why he should have strangled your wife?
> *A:* No, I can't.
> *Q:* Can you suggest why he should have strangled your daughter?
> *A:* No.

Christmas Humphreys sat down.

Evans was convicted. His appeal was dismissed and the execution date was set for 10 March. On 9 March Pierrepoint and his assistant, Syd Dernley, made their preparations in Pentonville. This is how Syd Dernley described that afternoon in his memoirs: 'The reception they gave him was amazing; everyone seemed to know him and to everyone he was "Albert". I lost count of the number of times I heard "Afternoon, Albert" as we passed screws and prison personnel … Pierrepoint was quite incredible. He had an air of professionalism and assurance about him that I never saw equalled by any other hangman.' Syd goes on to recall what happened on the morning of 10 March: 'Then, with only a few moments to go, Pierrepoint did something quite extraordinary. He reached into his bag and brought out a packet of cigars. The screw and I watched in disbelief as he carefully selected one and lit it. He smoked for perhaps a minute, no more, before they came for us. Pierrepoint stood up and rested the cigar, still burning, on an ashtray. He then walked through the door on his way to the execution.'

According to Syd, when they entered the condemned cell Evans looked straight at him: 'For the first time in my life I was looking directly at a truly terrified man.' Syd calculated that the execution took fifteen seconds. 'The doctor carried out his check and we returned to our quarters. Pierrepoint walked over to the ashtray and picked up his cigar. He drew on it and then slowly blew out a stream of smoke. It was still alight! I was impressed, as it was intended I should be. It was a little trick that I was to see him repeat many times, a boast about himself and his nerve and his speed.'

After the execution, Mr and Mrs Christie continued to live in the ground-floor flat at 10 Rillington Place. In March 1953 Christie moved out (Mrs Christie had not been seen since the previous December; according to Christie she had gone to Sheffield, or perhaps Birmingham). While the flat was empty, one of the upstairs lodgers was given permission to use Christie's kitchen. He cleared out all the rubbish and cleaned the kitchen. Knocking a nail into the kitchen wall to put up some brackets, he discovered that the wall was not a wall at all, but an alcove that had been papered over. Peeling back the paper, he saw a dead body. There were three bodies concealed behind the paper – the bodies of three prostitutes whom Christie had killed in the last three months. Underneath the floorboards in the front room was the body of Mrs Christie, whom Christie had killed in December 1952. All four women had been strangled.

The remains of two more women were discovered in the back garden and Christie confessed to murdering them in 1944, while he was working as a Special Constable. In the summer of that year, while his wife was visiting her family in Sheffield, he had brought a young Austrian girl back to the flat at 10 Rillington Place. She was a trained nurse, working in a munitions factory, and when she met Christie she may have been working part-time as a prostitute to supplement her income. According to Christie, he strangled her while they were having sex. Once she was dead he sexually abused her and then buried her body in the back garden. He said that in October 1944 he had murdered a second woman in a similar fashion, again burying her body in the back garden. This time he had used a home-made inhalation device to render his victim partially unconscious before he killed her. (It is important to understand that Christie was not only a murderer but also a necrophile.) Christie had committed these murders four years before Timothy and Beryl Evans moved into the upstairs flat at 10 Rillington Place.

Christie was put on trial for the murder of his wife. He did not deny killing any of the six women whose bodies had been found at 10 Rillington Place, but he pleaded not guilty on the basis of insanity. He said that he had murdered his wife as a mercy killing because she was ill and wanted to die. When he was asked about the women whose bodies were found in the garden and behind the wallpaper, he said that he had murdered them for sexual reasons, and that he had penetrated them as he was strangling them and when they were dead. He also said that he had strangled Beryl Evans in 1949, but denied killing her baby.

During Christie's trial the prosecuting counsel asked Chief Inspector Griffin about the Evans case:

> *Q:* Have you any reason for believing from your enquiries that the wrong man was hung in the case of Evans?
> *A:* None.

Christie did not appeal against his conviction for murder, but he did apply to the Home Secretary for a reprieve. In July 1953, while Maxwell Fyfe was considering Christie's case, he came under increasing pressure from MPs to hold a public inquiry to establish whether there had been a miscarriage of justice in the Evans case. He was very reluctant but eventually he appointed another lawyer, John Scott Henderson QC, to hold an inquiry. It lasted eleven days, it was held in private, and the barrister appointed to represent the interests of the Evans family was not allowed access to all the evidence. The Home Secretary refused all requests to debate the findings of the inquiry before Christie was executed and he refused to publish the transcript of the evidence given to the inquiry. On 13 July the Home Secretary announced that Christie's plea for clemency had been rejected – he would be executed on 15 July.

On 14 July the inquiry's report was published. This was the conclusion of John Scott Henderson QC, who led the inquiry: 'There is no ground for thinking that there may have been any miscarriage of justice in the conviction of Evans for the murder of Geraldine Evans.' He was satisfied that there could be no doubt that Evans was responsible for the deaths of his baby *and* his wife, and that Christie's statement that he was responsible for the death of Mrs Evans was untrue. It was an absurd conclusion.

In the parliamentary debate that followed, Geoffrey Bing QC demanded a proper public inquiry:

> The inquiry arose because it subsequently turned out that in Evans's case the principal witness for the Crown was found to have murdered six women in exactly the same way as he had, in the witness box, by implication, accused Evans of murdering two female persons. Quite apart from any confession, or absence of confession, it would be a really extraordinary coincidence that there should be two killers, killing their victims in exactly the same way, hiding them, as it turned out, in exactly the same place, and acting completely independently of each other. This is what Mr Scott Henderson found had taken place … when one looks at the second coincidence one finds that it is the even more remarkable one that Evans, without knowing anything about any of the murders committed by Christie … nevertheless chose to accuse, just by chance – and that is Mr Scott Henderson's case – the one person, probably in the whole of London at the time, who was murdering people in exactly the same way.

Sydney Silverman pushed home the point:

> There is an inevitable bias in the minds of all of us … to believe that what was done and what cannot be recalled was rightly done … If it were established in this case, as I for myself believe it has been established, that a man totally innocent of the crime with

> which he was charged was nevertheless executed, it is impossible to believe or assert that that would not result in some undermining of public confidence in the administration of justice ... We can survive the proof that an error was made. But there is one thing that the administration of justice will never survive, and that is if people begin to doubt not its infallibility but its integrity. That is where the damage is done ... if we allow people to believe that, having made the error, all the resources of the community are being employed to hush it up and deny it, then indeed confidence in the administration of justice will be undermined in such a way that it can never recover.

Maxwell Fyfe listened to the arguments and stuck to his guns: 'I do not believe there is a scintilla to support the attack on the motives and methods of Mr Scott Henderson.' There would not be another inquiry. Reginald Paget was incandescent:

> Let us put this perfectly plainly. This is not the last that this House ... will hear about the case of Timothy John Evans. Evans's mother, who is a devout Catholic, desires the body of her son to be taken to consecrated ground. It is the body of an innocent man, and it is entitled to be interred in consecrated ground. We shall not leave this matter, whatever Government is in power. We will raise it and raise it until that body is put at rest in holy ground.

Reginald Paget was right: the Evans case did not go away. MPs and investigative journalists continued to call for a public inquiry, although for years their campaign was largely ignored. In 1955 James Chuter-Ede MP added his voice to the campaign: 'I was the Home Secretary who wrote on Evans's papers, "The law must take its course." I never said, in 1948, that a mistake was impossible. I think Evans's case shows, in spite of all that has been done since, that a mistake was possible.' Chuter-Ede had revised his views on capital punishment as a result of the Evans case and he joined forces with those who called upon the Government to grant Evans a posthumous free pardon and allow him a proper burial.

In 1956, just after his resignation, an article by Pierrepoint was published in *Empire News*: 'I was sure with Christie, as I am sure with Evans, that they were guilty men, both of them ... I am absolutely sure that he [Evans] was guilty. I have seen so many murderers die, and there is something in the way their eyes meet mine, a flicker of a half-ashamed grimace that most of them give me.' Pierrepoint wanted the men he hanged to be guilty. Although he maintained that it was not his job to judge the condemned prisoners, that he was a cog in the machine, doing his sacred duty without fear or favour, the reality was different. Home Secretaries were fallible human beings and they made mistakes; they had to live with those mistakes, but they also had all the advantages and consolations of high office. They could immerse themselves in the fast-flowing waters of public life. Pierrepoint did not have that luxury; all he was left with was the memory of the fear in a stranger's eyes. Afterwards, he returned to a quiet house and a quiet wife. Albert Pierrepoint, the avuncular, cigar-smoking publican, was not going to entertain his regulars with stories of sending innocent men to their deaths. They needed to be guilty.

Ludovic Kennedy's book about the Evans case was published

in 1961. In the preface Kennedy made a personal plea to the Home Secretary (R. A. Butler): 'Can you, after reading this book, put your hand on your heart and say with Mr Scott Henderson that *there can be no doubt* that Evans murdered his wife and child?' The book mounted an extremely persuasive argument for Evans's innocence. It contained material which had never been made public before including, most significantly, an extract from the written instructions to Evans's barrister, prepared by his solicitors before the trial. These instructions referred to evidence about the examination of Beryl Evans given by the Home Office pathologist, Dr Teare, in the Magistrates' Court: 'The evidence given by Dr Teare appears to be open to the comment that his expert opinion travelled beyond justifiable inference from his examination of the corpse, in so far as he purports to suggest that there might have been an attempt at sexual penetration after death. The case is sufficiently horrible without disgusting surmises of this kind being introduced into the minds of the jury.'

At the time of the Evans trial this evidence could only have been damaging to Evans, although with the benefit of hindsight it is clearly fatal for Christie. As Ludovic Kennedy says. 'Not even those tortuous minds who believe that there were two stranglers living in the same house can believe that they were both necrophiles too.' The Home Secretary did not set up an inquiry to consider this evidence. Three years later an abolitionist Labour government was elected and still no inquiry was announced, despite the fact that the new Home Secretary had, when in opposition, called for one. Finally, in August 1965, the Home Secretary relented. In November 1965 the death penalty was suspended for five years (never to be re-introduced) and the public inquiry into the Evans case began. In the same month

Evans's body was exhumed and re0buried in St Patrick's cemetery in Leytonstone.

Sir Daniel Brabin, a High Court judge, delivered his report in October 1966: 'I have come to the conclusion that it is more probable than not that Evans killed Beryl Evans. I have come to the conclusion that it is more probable than not that Evans did not kill Geraldine.' This was unexpected. Whatever the disagreements about *who* had murdered Beryl and Geraldine, everyone involved in the case was in agreement that the same person had committed both murders. (Syd Dernley was quite frank about his reaction to the Brabin report: 'I was relieved.' He goes on to say that in his opinion both men were guilty of both murders. Perhaps from a professional point of view this was the most comforting conclusion he could reach.) Despite his peculiar findings, Sir Daniel Brabin did state in his report that no jury, knowing what was now known, would convict Evans of the murder of either his wife or his daughter. That was enough for Roy Jenkins, the new Home Secretary; on 18 October 1966 Jenkins announced that the Queen, on his recommendation, had granted Evans a posthumous free pardon. It had taken thirteen years.

CHAPTER NINE

Ruth Ellis

The Ruth Ellis story is not one story but many; it is the story of a young woman who murdered her lover, the story of her trial, which lasted just one and a half days, and the story of the Home Secretary who refused her plea for clemency. It is the story of how Albert Pierrepoint hanged her and what that hanging meant for him, for the whole country and for the future of capital punishment. Finally, it is a story about stories; about how we make up the story of our past and what we think it says about us.

Pierrepoint hanged Ruth Ellis at nine o'clock in the morning on 13 July 1955 at Holloway prison. Pierrepoint was fifty years old and Ellis was twenty-eight. *The Times* reported that on the morning of the execution a thousand people waited outside the prison. 'The crowd remained silent, with some people praying, as the execution hour at 9 a.m. passed. Eighteen minutes later the notices of execution were posted and the crowd rushed forward, blocking the road and halting the traffic. Police moved them back into two orderly queues and they filed past the notices on the prison gates.' The *Evening News* added more detail: 'As the chimes of Big Ben striking nine o'clock echoed from a radio in a house nearby the crowd of more than 800 stood bareheaded. The only sound came from the moving traffic and from a violinist playing in a side street. It was Bach's "Be Thou With Me when I Die"."

This is a quintessentially English story. Sleazy drinking clubs, peroxide hostesses in sequined dresses, weak-chinned men with money and silly moustaches, mansion house flats and black cabs. Sex, death and, of course, class. If it had happened in France there might have been more sex and less death (Ellis would not have died – no one could be hanged for a crime of passion in France). If it had happened in Italy there might have been more sex and more death (the Mafia would surely have been involved). There is something typically English, too, about the style of this story. It was not a grand, voluptuous tragedy; Ellis was not a great beauty and her lover was not a glamorous playboy but a former public school boy who looked a bit like Prince Charles and was no good at racing cars. The story was pinched, cut meanly at the seams. Not a classic tragedy of love scorned but a nasty, alcohol-sodden, pill-ridden mess that ended in violent death.

The facts, like most facts, are slippery. There is the evidence that was heard by the jury at the Old Bailey on 21 and 22 June 1955, but during the last fifty years dozens of articles, books and documentaries have produced new witnesses, new theories and new evidence. Amidst this continuing flurry of claim and counter-claim a few more or less stable facts have emerged. Ellis was born in Rhyl, North Wales, on 9 October 1926. Her father was a professional musician and her mother had come to England from Belgium during the First World War. Ellis was their fourth child. During the 1920s her father worked as a professional cellist, playing on board the ocean liners that sailed between Liverpool and New York or accompanying the silent movies in the cinemas of Rhyl, but his work dried up with the arrival of the talkies in the early 1930s. The family became poor, and moved around the country in search of work.

At this point Ellis's story becomes the story of the girl who got away, or tried to. Exactly what she was getting away from is buried in the shifting sands of family myth and memory. Poverty and dreariness, almost certainly. Her father, most probably. According to a book written by his granddaughter, Georgie Ellis, Arthur was a loving father and husband, transformed by poverty and drink into a violent alcoholic. According to a book written by his eldest daughter, Muriel Jakubait, Arthur abused and raped both her and Ellis. Both women agree that Ellis wanted to escape from the limitations of her family and her background. To begin with she escaped onto the dancefloor of the Streatham Locarno, where she was a great hit. At the age of seventeen, when her son Andre was born, she became a single mother. Andre's father was a Canadian soldier who returned to his wife and children. Andre was cared for by Ellis's older sister Muriel Jakubait, while Ellis worked as a nude model for the camera club and then as a hostess.

She met and married George Ellis in November 1950 when she was twenty-four. He was a forty-one-year-old dentist and a violent alcoholic. Soon after the marriage George became an inpatient at a mental hospital where he was treated, unsuccessfully, for his alcoholism. At around the same time Ellis was seen at the same hospital and given medication for depression, which she continued to take on and off for the rest of her life. Ellis was working while she was living with George, trying out a variety of more or less glamorous jobs. According to her sister, it was in the spring of 1951 that Ellis had her first and last film role, a non-speaking part in the fantastically named *Lady Godiva Rides Again*. The film is a satire on the world of beauty contests, following the fortunes of a would-be beauty queen, played by Pauline Stroud.

The line-up of contestants with lovely thighs included Kay Kendall, Joan Collins and Diana Dors. Further down this line there is a pretty brunette: it is Ellis in her pre-platinum days, at a time when she was four months pregnant with her second child, Georgie, and in the midst of a life with George that was dominated by serious domestic violence. Seven smiling lovelies stand between Ellis and Diana Dors. They are all in swimwear and high heels; some have flowers in their hair, some are wearing large hats. The swimwear is tight – shiny satin straining over fashionably rounded stomachs – but only Diana Dors, in a risqué tropical bikini, is showing her navel. (This was too much for an American audience, and the film was banned there.) Dors was nineteen at the time, five years younger than Ellis, and, like Ellis, she was hoping for greater things. Unlike Ellis, she got them, at least temporarily. When the film was finished Diana Dors married Dennis Price and became a figure on the London club scene, an early tabloid celebrity. In 1955, the year when Pierrepoint executed Ellis, Dors was at the Venice Film Festival, posing in a mink and diamond bikini to publicise her new film, *Yield to the Night*, about a young blonde woman awaiting execution.

By the autumn of 1953 Ellis was working as the manageress of another club in Knightsbridge, called the Little Club. It was run by the notorious 'vice boss' Morris Conley, who owned a number of clubs and brothels where the line between barmaid and prostitute was conveniently blurred. Ellis was separated from George Ellis but they were not divorced. She had recently started a relationship with David Blakely, who was three years younger than her. Blakely was the son of a doctor, educated at Shrewsbury. When he met Ellis he was engaged to be married to a woman whose background was similar to his own, and he was having an affair with a third woman, who was married. He was a dedicated but unsuccessful racing car driver and a womaniser with no regular income. Soon after they met he moved into the flat above the Little Club where Ellis was living with her children.

The relationship between Ellis and Blakely lasted for nineteen months. It was characterised by drinking, sexual passion, infidelity and violence. Both drank heavily, both were sexually passionate and both were unfaithful. Only Blakely was violent. Towards the end of 1953 Ellis became pregnant and had an abortion. The following year Ellis agreed to the informal adoption of her daughter, Georgie, by a well-to-do couple with no children who lived in Warrington. Georgie was three and a half years old when her mother was executed and eight years old when she found out that her mother had been executed. In 1954 Ellis met an older man and in the summer of that year she had an affair with him whilst Blakely was racing cars in Le Mans. Desmond Cussen came from a successful business background, had a flat in Marylebone and drove a black cab for pleasure. The affair was probably short-lived, but Cussen continued to play an important part in Ellis's life. He became a financial and moral support to Ellis, disapproving of Blakely's violence and infidelity. The scene became increasingly claustrophobic – Ellis was employed by Conley at the Little Club to be professionally charming, and both Cussen and Blakely spent hours in the club, drinking and steadily fermenting their sexual jealousy. It is one of the hallmarks of this story that none of the leading characters, with the exception of Ellis, had much work to keep them occupied.

In December 1954 Ellis lost her job as manageress of the Little Club. Ellis and her son Andre moved in with Cussen. Ellis didn't have to pay any rent and she regularly spent nights in hotels with Blakely. In January 1955 Ellis received the decree nisi in her divorce from George Ellis and this meant that she would soon be free to marry Blakely. The relationship was still punctuated by serious violence, infidelity and drunken scenes, but they had both spoken about the possibility of marriage. By March Ellis was living in a one-bedroom flat, paid for by Cussen, and Blakely stayed with her regularly. Andre was at boarding school, also paid for by Cussen, and slept on a camp bed in his mother's bedroom during the holidays.

In March Ellis discovered that she was pregnant, but at the end of the month Blakely punched her hard in the stomach and she almost certainly miscarried as a result of this assault. In the first week of April Blakely gave Ellis a photograph of himself, signed, 'To Ruth, with all my love, David.' It was an official racing team photograph, important to Blakely because it marked a degree of professional success. The pro-Ellis camp say that Ellis attached huge importance to the giving of this photograph as a measure of what she believed to be Blakely's new commitment to her.

It is clear that Blakely left Ellis's flat on the morning of 8 April 1955 and spent the day with friends in Hampstead, the Findlaters. But no one knows whether they parted well. One version is that when Blakely left on Friday morning he was loving and kind, and the couple agreed to meet on Friday evening.

The alternative version is that Blakely escaped to his friends' house because he couldn't stand Ellis a moment longer and needed their help in ending the relationship.

In the evening Ellis attempted to contact Blakely at his friends' house. She spoke to Findlater on the phone and he told her that Blakely wasn't there. Later that evening Ellis asked Cussen to drive her to Hampstead and they saw Blakely's car parked outside the Findlaters' house. Ellis rang the doorbell and then phoned the house from a phone box nearby; someone answered the phone and hung up. Ellis took a heavy rubber torch from Cussen's car and used it to push in the windows of Blakely's car. Findlater called the police and eventually they persuaded Ellis to leave. Cussen drove her home. Early the next morning, which was a Saturday, Ellis returned to Hampstead and hid in a doorway near the Findlaters' house, from where she saw Blakely and Findlater emerging at about 10 a.m. Ellis, with Cussen as her driver, spent most of the day following Blakely, secretly observing his movements and trying to speak to him on the phone. All her attempts to speak to him directly were thwarted, mostly by Findlater. By this time Ellis believed that Blakely was sleeping with another woman at the Findlaters' house.

On Easter Sunday, 10 April, Ellis telephoned the Findlaters' house at 9 a.m. Again she was prevented from speaking to Blakely. The events of Sunday afternoon are literally unfathomable, concealed in the muddy waters of competing versions; however, it is incontrovertible that Ellis did return to the Findlaters' house on Sunday evening. Blakely's car was not outside their house so she went straight to the local pub to look for him. His car was parked outside the Magdala pub. Ellis watched through the window while Blakely and a friend bought cigarettes and beer from the off-licence counter. When they emerged Ellis took a gun out of her handbag and shot Blakely four times. He was taken by ambulance to the nearby New End hospital and was pronounced dead on arrival. Ellis was taken to Hampstead police station. Thirteen weeks later she was executed by Pierrepoint.

These are the bare bones of the story. Hours after her arrest Ellis was interviewed by the police and made a statement admitting that she had shot Blakely. She described the day of the murder and what she did before she went to Hampstead to find Blakely. This is the crucial sentence: 'When I put the gun in my bag I intended to find David and shoot him.' It was a textbook admission to murder. Two days later, on 12 April 1955, Ellis wrote a letter to Blakely's mother:

> Dear Mrs Cook,
> No dought [*sic*] these last few days have been a shock to you. Please try to believe me, when I say, how deeply sorry I am to have caused you this unpleasantness.
>
> No dought you will know all kinds of stories regarding David and I. Please do forgive him for deceiving you, has [*sic*] regarding myself.
>
> David and I have spent many happy times together.
>
> Thursday 7th April, David arrived home at 7.15 p.m., he gave me the latest photograph he had, a few days hence had taken, he told me had given you one.
>
> Friday morning at 10 o'clock he left and promised to return at 8 o'clock, but never did. The two people I blame for David's death, and my own, are the

> Finlayters [*sic*]. No dought you will not understand this but perhaps before I hang you will know what I mean.
>
> Please excuse my writing, but the pen is shocking.
>
> I implore you to try and forgive David for living with me, but we were very much in love with one and other [*sic*] unfortunately David was not satisfied with one woman in his life.
>
> I have forgiven David, I only wish I could have found it in my heart to have forgiven when he was alive.
>
> Once again, I say I am very sorry to have caused you this misery and heartache.
>
> I shall die loving your son, and you should feel content that his death has been repaid.
>
> Goodbye.
>
> Ruth Ellis

This letter has been quoted in every book about Ellis. It is a familiar item in the macabre gallery of true crime artefacts, called in aid of whatever position the writer happens to take on the Ellis case; the disordered thoughts of a mind in crisis can be extracted and used to support almost anything. It proves how deeply Ellis loved Blakely, it proves that she had no remorse, it proves that she always knew that she was going to hang. And so on. When I first read it, my initial reaction was a sense of shock that the most private of letters had been made public. But I think I was shocked more by the contents of the letter than by the fact that I was allowed to read it. It was so banal, so hopeless, so muddled. The words Ellis chose seemed to have no relationship to the thing she was describing. Just as Ellis had done something that had caused 'unpleasantness' for Blakely's mother, so Pierrepoint had a 'sacred' duty to perform for Ellis. Ellis relies on euphemism to sanitise her act of violence, and Pierrepoint, the Edwardian, relies on religion to sanitise his. In the words of the historian Arthur Marwick, the 1950s was the era of 'emollient fibbing'. Pierrepoint and Ellis were both good at it.

On 12 April Ellis appeared at the Hampstead Magistrates' Court, where she was remanded in custody and taken to Holloway to await trial. The trial was listed for the end of June and Ellis's solicitor, John Bickford, did not have long to prepare. Solicitors are supposed to act in the best interests of their client, and often that involves issues that have nothing at all to do with the law; on page six of John Bickford's 'Supplementary Brief to Counsel for the Accused' is the sub-heading: Accused's personal appearance.' John Bickford sets out the background:

> Efforts have been made to enable the Accused to have her hair attended to because it is now changing colour patchily as a result of continued neglect ... but the Governor has stated that she has no authority to grant such a request. An interview is being sought with the Governor in order to see what can be done: it is submitted that it is of considerable importance to the Accused that she should be able to look her best at the trial and if she were on a charge which admitted of bail there would not be any difficulty to enable her to be attended to ... Counsel's views are sought as to what steps ought to be taken for the purpose.

The Governor was persuaded and when Ellis appeared in the

dock at the Old Bailey her hair was newly done, the dye supplied by her own hairdressers: Sak's of Shaftesbury Avenue.

The hair dye is important because it has become part of the Ruth Ellis story. All the newspaper reports of the trial opened with a description of Ellis's physical appearance. At best she was brassy, or immaculate platinum; at worst she was a blonde tart. The newspapers described her clothes in some detail: the black two-piece suit with an astrakhan collar and the white blouse. In the books about the Ellis case, some of them published twenty years or more after the event, Ellis continues to be brassy and immaculate, the suit is still a two-piece and the shirt is still a blouse. Almost without exception, these later accounts of the trial describe Ellis in the courtroom in terms of an actress on the West End stage, making her grand debut. We, the reader, know that tragically, thrillingly, her debut will also be her final curtain call. She doesn't know how this play will end. Or perhaps she does – perhaps she believes that she will leave this earthly stage to be reunited with her beloved Blakely. Ellis has become the tragic heroine of the post-war era, petrified in period detail, living and breathing in black and white, with a slash of red around the lips. The urge to retell the story as a 1950s B-movie melodrama seems almost irresistible. The brassy blouse defines her; she is feisty but fast, the tart who is going to the gallows with her attitude intact. Fifty years on it is easy to think of the Ellis case in these terms – a kind of heritage horror.

This heritage horror ignores the reality, which was much more complicated. In the early 1950s, class distinctions were changing but they were still important; the social and economic position of women was changing but there was still an expectation that women should perform a maternal and domestic role within a traditional family structure. The forces of conservatism were engaged in a losing battle with the forces of change, but the battle had not yet been lost. Ellis was a divorcee, a single working mother with two children from different fathers and two lovers. She had had an abortion and one of her children had been placed voluntarily with another family. She had been subjected to serious and repeated physical violence. She had taken her clothes off to earn a living at the camera club and she had worked in a drinking club where women could accept money for sex if they chose to. The men she met in the clubs were from the middle and upper classes. Both her lovers were public school boys. Illegitimate births and divorce rates were both on the increase, and prostitution was becoming more visible and more politically sensitive. At the same time that Ellis was hostessing at Carroll's, where the businessmen stayed until 3 a.m. and watched the cabaret or danced with the girls, the British Vigilance Association was campaigning for the suppression of criminal vice and against the exploitation of prostitution and public immorality. Ellis was the product and the victim of a moment of tremendous social flux. Her trial at the Old Bailey lasted just one and a half days and it could be described as an open and shut case: she had shot her lover at close range, in cold blood. What could be simpler?

CHAPTER TEN

Trial and Execution

Ellis's case was listed for trial at the Old Bailey on 20 June 1955. The press were out in force, including the foreign press, fascinated and horrified in equal measure by the possibility that a young woman might be sentenced to death for a crime of passion. Pierrepoint was the 'number one' hangman. The execution of a woman was a rare event and most executioners were reluctant to do it. Pierrepoint, however, did not mind. Only four women had been executed in England since 1936, all of them by Pierrepoint. From the moment the case was first reported Pierrepoint knew that if she was convicted, and if there was no reprieve, he would receive a letter from the Sheriff requesting his presence at Holloway prison to execute Ruth Ellis.

It is not possible to understand the Ellis trial without looking first at the weeks leading up to it. When a jury is sworn in at the beginning of a criminal trial they become part of a judicial drama. They are the audience; watching, listening, and then pronouncing their verdict. But they do not know the dramatic conventions governing the play and they are not familiar with its language. The jury must determine whether the defendant is innocent or guilty on the basis of the evidence that is before them, and nothing else. What the judge does not tell them is that the evidence they have heard is just one of many versions of what has happened, that there were a number of earlier drafts, all of which would have made a slightly different play. The evidence is like a script and it has been carefully drafted and redrafted by the police and the lawyers over the preceding weeks and months.

The initial creative force behind this production are the police – how they conduct the investigation, which lines of inquiry they pursue and which they leave out, will determine the essential quality of the final performance. In the Ellis case it was Detective Chief Inspector Davies who submitted twenty-six witness statements and his own report to the Director of Public Prosecutions. This is what he said at the conclusion of his report: 'This is clearly a case of jealousy on the part of Ellis, coupled with the fear that Blakely was leaving her. In spite of what Cussen says, that Ellis wanted to be rid of Blakely and he would not leave, the weight of the evidence points quite clearly to the position being completely reversed. The two people, Blakely and Ellis, are of completely different stations in life.' (The 1953 Report of the Royal Commission on Capital Punishment included various statistical tables designed to show who was being murdered. Cases were divided into categories: murder of parent, murder of police or prison officer, and so on. These categories included wife, mistress, lover and sweetheart. Presumably David Blakely was a lover. If it had been the other way round, would Ellis have been his sweetheart, or his lover? Did 'sweetheart' imply an engagement, or just a certain degree of propriety?)

When the prosecution see the police statements there is another rewrite. The prosecution lawyers may want more evidence to strengthen their case or they may not like all the evidence that the police have gathered – there may be material that they do not want the jury or even the defence lawyers to see. Once the defence have some idea of the evidence they will also want to make changes, and if the lawyers cannot reach agreement on exactly what evidence should go before the jury, the judge will decide. These legal arguments are heard by the judge in the absence of the jury, either in earlier court hearings or during the trial itself, when the jury are asked to leave the courtroom while the barristers and the judge discuss a 'point of law'. The jury are only allowed to see the finished version of the script and they are required to accept it as the only version. They cannot ask to see an earlier draft and if they suspect that some lines have been cut they are supposed to dismiss their suspicions. These are the rules of evidence and they create a necessary fiction which underpins the whole jury system. A trial can be perfectly fair, in the sense that it has been properly conducted according to the rules of law and evidence, and yet it can appear to be terribly unfair in the ordinary sense of the word. This, I think, is what happened in the Ellis trial. There was nothing technically wrong with the process and yet, with hindsight, it seems shockingly unjust.

Within hours of being taken to Hampstead police station on the night of 10 April, Ellis had made a full statement. It was very late at night and she was in shock, but there is nothing to suggest either that the police broke any rules or that they acted with any malice. Taking a statement in these circumstances would not have been considered wrong or surprising at the time, although from a twenty-first-century standpoint it seems almost incredible that Ellis made a detailed statement before she had seen a solicitor and, even worse, before she had been charged with anything. In 1955 there weren't many rules governing the conduct of police inquiries and there seemed to be little reason to restrain the police in the exercise of their powers. The statement was really a confession, not a statement at all. Crucially, in this statement Ellis said that the gun she had used to shoot Blakely had been given to her about three years earlier in the club by somebody whose name she did not know, as security for a loan. She also said that no one else had been involved in the shooting. It was a terribly important issue because if someone had given her the gun in the knowledge that she planned to use it to shoot Blakely, that person could have been charged with Ellis as an accessory or even as a principal. That would undoubtedly have had an impact on the trial and it could well have led to a different verdict.

Ellis's explanation of how she got the gun was extremely unconvincing and no one, including the police, her own lawyers and the judge, believed it. Despite this, her explanation was not challenged at the trial because there was no evidence to support an alternative explanation. Before the trial the police took a statement from a witness who suggested that Cussen owned a gun similar to the one used in the killing. The police questioned Cussen and he said that he had never owned a revolver. He showed the police a starter pistol and an air pistol which he kept in his flat, and suggested that the witness might have mistaken them for a revolver. Cussen maintained that on the day of the murder he had taken Ellis and her son Andre home at 7.30 p.m. and had not seen her again until after her arrest. The police didn't find any other evidence linking Cussen to the gun, and at her trial Ellis gave the same explanation that she had given in her statement to the police on the night of the murder.

What about the defence lawyers? Why didn't they get to the

bottom of the gun story? Ellis's solicitor, John Bickford, instructed a QC and two junior barristers to represent her at the Old Bailey, and the files at the Public Record Office are full of his briefs to counsel. Briefs, supplementary briefs and appendices. Page after page of instructions. Bickford clearly spent a lot of time on this case and he was under a lot of pressure. It was a high profile case that would be hard to win. When Bickford first met Ellis she told him that she wanted to plead guilty to murder and that she believed in the principle of a life for a life. More than that, she wanted to be with Blakely in the afterlife. Her junior barrister, Peter Rawlinson, who later became Attorney General, recalled the same desperate attitude in his autobiography. He spoke to Ellis in the cells after a preliminary hearing to fix the date of her trial: ' "You will make certain, won't you," she said quietly, "that I shall be hanged? That is the only way I can join him." I caught my breath and said that she must not talk like that. But she shook her head and repeated, "I want to join him. I want to join him." ' Bickford eventually persuaded Ellis to enter a not guilty plea, but he couldn't persuade her to change her unconvincing story about the gun. It seemed that she wanted to take full responsibility for killing Blakely.

In 1955 there were four possible defences to a charge of murder: firstly, entering a plea of not guilty by virtue of insanity (Ellis was obviously not insane); secondly, proving that the defendant did not commit the act itself (not possible – she clearly did); thirdly, proving that the defendant acted in self-defence (again not possible – she clearly did not); and lastly, establishing that there was sufficient evidence of provocation to allow the jury to consider an alternative verdict of guilty to manslaughter instead of murder. In 1957, partly in response to the Ellis case, the Homicide Act introduced the legal concept of diminished responsibility, allowing the jury to return a verdict of manslaughter instead of murder if the defendant could prove that at the time of the killing she was suffering from an abnormality of mind serious enough to impair her mental responsibility. But in 1955 the only realistic option for Ellis was to argue that Blakely's violence and infidelity and her jealousy combined to provoke her.

To make it even harder, before the jury could consider the question of provocation, the defence had first of all to convince the judge that, on the balance of probabilities, it was safe to leave the issue of provocation for the jury to decide. At that time provocation was defined by case law as an act, or acts, which would cause in any reasonable person 'a sudden and temporary loss of self-control, rendering the accused so subject to passion as to make him or her for the moment not master of his mind', which really means acting in the heat of the moment. The case law made it clear that a defendant could not have a sudden and temporary loss of control that lasted several weeks. The defence were in a difficult position, despite Blakely's persistent and vicious assaults on Ellis. They would have to show that Blakely's behaviour immediately before the killing was so terrible that killing him was a proportionate response. The fact that he had assaulted Ellis two weeks earlier was not relevant in law. Thirty years later the concept of cumulative or 'slow burn provocation' was recognised by the common law, providing a defence for women who had been subjected to persistent and serious violence by their partners. But given the state of the law in 1955, the defence of provocation was unlikely to succeed for Ellis. So perhaps no one was to blame and the verdict was inevitable?

Peter Rawlinson took this line in his autobiography: 'Her solicitor was John Bickford, a conscientious and kindly man who did all that could be done for her ... As the law stood in 1955 there could be no real defence on her behalf to the charge of murder. The leading counsel in our defence team, Melford Stevenson, could do little.'

Whether or not this is true, it is a predictable comment. The Bar is governed by lots of strange and unspoken rules, one being that a barrister should always be publicly supportive of another barrister. Fortunately, there is also a maverick tendency at the Bar and occasionally barristers like to break their own rules. The trial judge was Mr Justice Havers, father of Sir Michael Havers, who became Attorney General in 1979, and Dame Elizabeth Butler-Sloss, President of the Family Division of the High Court. When Mr Justice Havers was interviewed for a television documentary in 1977 he was asked if the defence in the Ellis case was weak. 'It was so weak, I think you could say it was non-existent.' For a judge, this is pretty strong stuff. Melford Stevenson QC became a High Court judge two years after defending Ellis and was known as an advocate of capital punishment and a tough trial judge. He tried the Kray twins and dined at the Garrick. A distinguished legal career.

Distinguished or not, Mr Justice Havers was right. The whole trial lasted just one and a half days, which is shockingly short for a murder trial, even a relatively uncomplicated one. A court might spend a day and a half on a very straightforward case of handling stolen goods, or perhaps possession of a small amount of drugs, but a murder trial usually takes at least a week and often much longer. The prosecution was led by Christmas Humphreys, another member of the Garrick, and a founding president of the Buddhist Society, the same man who had defended Pons and Kieboom during the war and had persuaded the jury to acquit Pons. He was now Senior Prosecuting Counsel at the Old Bailey, responsible for some of the most sensitive and difficult prosecutions of the period. (In his autobiography Humphreys explained how he had reconciled his religion with his job as a prosecutor of people who were liable to be sentenced to death:

> If it was my karma to prosecute, it was the karma of the prisoner not only to be prosecuted by me but also to have committed that crime or at least to be on trial for it ... And his death, if he were hanged, would be the result of *his* causing, and might, as it were, wipe out the causing in the infinitely complex, infinitely subtle weaving of this cosmic web ... We all die; we all come back, according to the law.

Christmas Humphreys died at the age of eighty-two, twenty-eight years after Ellis was hanged at the age of twenty-nine).

Melford Stevenson cross-examined just two out of the sixteen prosecution witnesses, Anthony Findlater and Desmond Cussen. Ellis was convinced that the Findlaters were somehow to blame for Blakely's death, and she wanted to expose them as malicious snobs who had come between herself and Blakely and encouraged his infidelity. She wanted Melford Stevenson to bring all this out in his cross-examination and to put Findlater in his place, to humiliate him. This was one of the reasons that she had agreed to plead not guilty. But when it came to it, Melford Stevenson's cross-examination of Findlater was brief and fairly courteous. Findlater refused to accept that during the weekend prior to the killing Ellis had been driven into a frenzy of suspicion and jealousy by Blakely's refusal to speak to her and the presence of a young nanny in the Findlater household.

Melford Stevenson's cross-examination of Desmond Cussen was equally restrained. He even seemed reluctant to elicit from Cussen any details about the injuries that Ellis had sustained as a result of Blakely's assaults: 'I do not want to press you for details, but how often have you seen that sort of mark on her?' At the conclusion of the prosecution case Melford Stevenson called the witnesses for the defence: Ellis herself and a psychologist who had examined Ellis in Holloway. His evidence was not just unhelpful to Ellis, it was positively damaging. The defence didn't produce any other medical evidence about Ellis's state of mind at the time of the killing, despite the fact that she had been drinking heavily and taking tranquillisers, which had been prescribed to her by a psychiatrist who had noted her tendency towards pathological jealousy.

The Ellis who appeared in the witness box refused to conform to anyone's idea of a wronged woman, or a woman in love, or a hysterical woman. Her demeanour was calm, she spoke little about her feelings, she was sexually confident and she did not want to be seen as a victim. Crucially, she did not say sorry. When she was asked about her first pregnancy by Blakely, Ellis told the jury that he had offered to marry her but she had refused: 'I was not really in love with him at that time, and it was quite unnecessary to marry me, I thought. I could get out of the mess quite easily.' It is impossible to imagine a reply that could have ingratiated her less with the jury – she was living with a man she didn't really love, she wasn't interested in marriage, the unborn baby was 'a mess' and an abortion something to be shrugged off casually. Famously, in cross-examination Ellis was asked just one question by Christmas Humphreys: 'Mrs Ellis, when you fired that revolver at close range into the body of David Blakely, what did you intend to do ?' To which she replied:

'It was obvious when I shot him I intended to kill him.' There are very few, if any, moments in a barrister's career when the witness they are cross-examining gives an answer that will inevitably condemn them. For Christmas Humphreys this was one of those moments.

When Ellis had completed her evidence Melford Stevenson made his submissions to the judge on the issue of provocation. He wanted the judge to allow the jury to decide whether Ellis was guilty of manslaughter, rather than murder, on the grounds of provocation. Mr Justice Havers adjourned overnight to consider the legal submissions and in the morning he ruled that there was not sufficient evidence of provocation for the issue to be left to the jury. This meant that the jury could not even consider whether or not Ellis was guilty of manslaughter rather than murder. They were left with just one decision – was Ellis guilty of murder? Melford Stevenson decided that in the circumstances there was no point making a closing speech to the jury, and Christmas Humphreys followed suit. The jury retired for twenty-three minutes before returning their verdict: guilty. There was no recommendation for mercy. Before sentencing Ellis, Mr Justice Havers was handed a small square of black material which he put on top of his wig. 'Ruth Ellis, the jury have convicted you of murder. In my view, it was the only possible verdict. The sentence of the Court upon you is that you shall be taken from this place to a lawful prison, and thence to a place of execution, and that you there suffer death by hanging.'

In one sense Melford Stevenson was not responsible for any of this. After all, Ellis didn't want to talk about Blakely's violence and she didn't want to say sorry. She wanted to expose the Findlaters and then join Blakely in another world. There is only so much that any barrister can do once their client is in the witness box. On the other hand, barristers regularly have to defend people who will almost certainly be found guilty, people who have given up and will do nothing to help themselves. It is the barrister's job to do everything possible to get their client off. In these hopeless cases it is more important than ever that the defendant feels that she has had a fair trial, a good run for her money. It is hard to see how Ellis could have felt this after one and a half days at the Old Bailey. It is also hard to understand why the defence did not make a better case for a recommendation of mercy. The defence of provocation had little chance of success, but a jury trial is always a game and tactics are important. Before the start of any trial the defence will make all kinds of tactical decisions about how they want to run their case. In 1955 it was open to a jury to find a defendant guilty of murder but to recommend mercy, and getting this recommendation was really Ellis's best bet. Despite this, the defence failed to put forward any evidence that, although not strictly relevant to the question of provocation, might have persuaded the jury to recommend mercy.

There was no evidence about Ellis's psychiatric history, no medical evidence about the injuries caused by Blakely's assaults and no evidence about her children. Whether or not Ellis herself wanted mercy, with hindsight it seems wrong that she was allowed to damn herself so quickly, without a real fight.

Why did Melford Stevenson only cross-examine two witnesses? And why was his cross-examination so brief? What happened to all those pages of instructions, so carefully prepared by John Bickford? In 1982, when he was seventy-nine years old, Melford Stevenson took part in a radio phone-in about capital punishment. He had always been an advocate of capital punishment and the presenter asked him if he thought justice had been done when Ellis was hanged: 'I'm afraid it was. But may I in justice to her say how I revere her memory. She was a splendid girl … I still remember most clearly that when she appeared at the Old Bailey her lovely blonde hair was perfectly dyed.' Pompous, patronising and self-serving, a particularly unattractive combination. It is tempting to dismiss Stevenson as a misogynistic toff whose behaviour in court was motivated by loyalty to his own class and sex, rather than by loyalty to his client. Ellis's behaviour was a challenge to the traditional, pre-war social order and already the newspapers had labelled her as a blonde tart. Stevenson could have given the jury another version of Ellis's story by exposing the full extent of Blakely's violence and infidelity, but he chose not to dwell on any unpleasantness because Blakely was a man and a member of his own class. This is the feminist analysis of the Ellis trial and it is a very persuasive one. In theory I agree with it, but my experience at the Bar forces me, reluctantly, to admit that in practice it might – only might – be overstated. It is possible that Stevenson's conduct of the case was *not* an expression of his own values and beliefs.

A barrister is a performer. He has to play to the jury if he is going to persuade them to acquit his client. Juries are unpredictable and they don't always do what they are told. They regularly acquit people in the face of what seems to be overwhelming evidence of guilt, perhaps because they feel sorry for the defendant, or because they don't like the police officer or because the defence barrister has made them laugh. At the beginning of every case the defence barrister has to make a leap in the dark; he has to decide who these twelve members of the jury are, what they are going to like and what they are going to hate, and he has to run his case according to that decision. So perhaps Melford Stevenson decided that if he went on the offensive, attacking Anthony Findlater and vilifying Blakely, he would alienate the jury. Perhaps he genuinely thought that the best tactic was to play it down and depend upon the jury's sympathy for a woman who had been betrayed. That would have been a perfectly sensible tactic, and it might have paid off.

Ellis was sentenced to death by Mr Justice Havers on 21 June 1955 and the execution date was set for 13 July. Now the only hope was to persuade the Home Secretary, Gwilym Lloyd-George, to grant a reprieve. Thousands were moved to support the campaign to save Ellis – questions were asked in Parliament, petitions were signed and newspapers called for a reprieve. William Connor in the *Daily Mirror* launched a scathing attack: 'You who read this paper – and millions like you – are the key supporters of this sickening system whereby with panoply and brutality mixed with the very dubious sauce of religion and consolation we bury our worst malefactors in the quick-lime grave … if we do it, and if we continue to do it to her sad successors, then we all bear the guilt of savagery untinged with mercy.'

The Government was inundated with letters and telegrams from around the world, some from the most unexpected places. On 8 July 1955 the Secretary of State for the Colonies received a telegram from the British Guiana Women's Social Labour Organisation, asking for a reprieve: 'Case aroused much interest in British Guiana. Motivated by jealousy of aggravated nature, brave front and prepared to bear consequences although penitent and surely mindful of reprieve. Consider children alone in world. Act of mercy will be great boon to international womanhood.' This was more than an irritating domestic battle between the Government and a vociferous but relatively small group of abolitionists; it was becoming a political embarrassment.

Two weeks before the date set for Ellis's execution, the police received a letter from a woman called Mrs Dyer, a close friend of Ellis who had worked with her at the Little Club. Mrs Dyer was French, married to an English doctor. In her letter she said that she had helped Ellis move a few months before the murder. She had packed all Ellis's belongings and she had not seen a gun. She also told them that during one of her visits to Ellis in Holloway prison, Ellis had told her that Cussen had given her the gun and driven her to Hampstead on the night of the murder.

After receiving Mrs Dyer's letter, Detective Chief Inspector Davies wrote a long memo to the Assistant Chief Constable setting out the history of the investigation of the gun issue: 'Ellis's story that she had the gun in her possession for three years was not believed from the outset because of the clean and well-oiled condition it was in.' He goes on to say that before the trial he had questioned Ellis several times about the gun: 'Throughout she was adamant that this story was true. In view of this we were forced to accept the fact that Cussen did not give a revolver to her.' Davies goes on to describe his meeting with Mrs Dyer: 'It is my opinion after seeing her [Mrs Dyer] that, being a French woman, she finds it difficult to believe that Ellis should pay the supreme penalty for a crime of this nature. I think she is genuine in her efforts to save her friend, but unfortunately she cannot say anything that we do not already know and that has been enquired into.' This is all rather puzzling; perhaps, being a well-brought-up Englishman, Detective Chief Inspector Davies did not want to suggest that Mrs Dyer was not being entirely truthful. It was better manners to ascribe her lack of credibility to her nationality.

On 11 July the Governor of Holloway prison, Dr Charity Taylor, told Ellis that the Home Secretary had refused a reprieve. The newspaper reports reached a fever pitch of voyeuristic claim and counter-claim – Ellis wanted to die, she didn't want to die, she was hysterical, she was calm and reading her Bible. Pierrepoint had lots of experience of condemned prisoners receiving a reprieve but usually there was little publicity. There had not been a public execution in England since 1868, but suddenly Pierrepoint found himself playing a leading role in a media event – this was the modern version of a public execution and Pierrepoint was forced into the limelight. It had happened once before, in 1945, when he had executed the Nazi war criminals, but then he had been treated with something verging on respect – an ambassador for the English way of hanging, performing an unpleasant but necessary public duty on behalf of the civilised world. By 1955 that had all been forgotten. Pierrepoint's part in the Ellis drama was much less respectable, much less wholesome.

On 11 July Ellis sacked John Bickford and asked to see her previous solicitor, Victor Mishcon, later Lord Mishcon. On 12 July Mishcon visited Ellis in Holloway and she made a statement in which she said that on the day of the killing she had been drinking large quantities of Pernod with Cussen, that Cussen had given her a gun and driven her to Hampstead. Ellis told Mishcon that she had no interest in a reprieve, but she did give him permission to show the statement to the Home Office. Mishcon said later that Ellis genuinely had no interest whatsoever in a reprieve and that he had persuaded her to make the statement by reminding her of her duty to her son Andre. He argued that Ellis owed it to her son to leave behind her own account of the murder; otherwise he would have to rely on what he read in the newspapers.

On 12 July Mishcon rushed off to the Home Office with the statement and sought an urgent meeting with the Permanent

Under-Secretary of State, Sir Frank Newsam. Pierrepoint was on his way from Preston to London, unsure whether he would be carrying out the execution the following morning. Sir Frank, meanwhile, was at Ascot and had to be tannoyed in the Royal Enclosure, much to the delight of the popular press: 'Drama of Ascot Race Bid to Save Ruth Ellis,' trumpeted the *Daily Sketch*. (There is a rather curious entry for Newsam in *The Dictionary of National Biography*: 'He had about him an aura of power and authority. In conversation, he would sometimes ... quote by heart some passage from Aeschylus. But he also drank quite a lot, was an inveterate gambler on horse-racing, and enjoyed dancing and social occasions.') Newsam's assistant, Philip Allen, began dealing with the case in the absence of his superior and he instructed the police to look for Desmond Cussen. He also had to consider more evidence about Ellis's new statement. A prison officer who had been present during the meeting between Ellis and Mishcon made a statement which claimed that Ellis had told Mishcon that it was *her* idea to take a gun, not Cussen's idea, as the Mishcon statement had implied. Newsam looked at the two statements and noted that the discrepancy was 'interesting and illuminating'. But, as Mishcon commented in a BBC interview forty-four years later, 'With great respect, he didn't allow much time for the light to illuminate.'

The police started looking for Cussen at 4.30 p.m. on 12 July. At the same time, according to the *Daily Express*, the 200-strong crowd outside Holloway fell silent as Pierrepoint arrived at the gates of the prison in a taxi. Later the same afternoon Pierrepoint made his calculations and prepared the equipment. He worked quietly in the execution chamber just yards from Ellis's cell, adjusting the length of the drop and leaving the rope overnight with a sandbag tied at the end, so that it would be stretched for the morning. At midnight the police were instructed to stop their search for Cussen. Why was the search abandoned so quickly? The Home Secretary could have ordered a temporary stay of execution to allow more time to investigate the new evidence and to find Cussen, but he chose not to do so. In practice a temporary stay would have made it impossible for the Government to withstand the pressure for a reprieve. If Ellis was reprieved, after shooting a man repeatedly at close range, who could be hanged? In the words of a memo written by Gwilym Lloyd-George, 'If a reprieve were granted in this case, we should have seriously to consider whether capital punishment should be retained as a penalty.' The Government was not yet willing to consider abolition. Pierrepoint was still in business.

CHAPTER ELEVEN

Afterlife

On 13 July 1955 Pierrepoint left Holloway prison with a police escort. He was pursued by reporters to Euston station where he got the train back to his home in Preston. The day after the execution a wax effigy of Ellis appeared in Louis Tussaud's Chamber of Horrors in Blackpool. The figure was dressed in a black evening gown, not the smart black two-piece suit with an astrakhan collar that Ellis wore at her trial, the subject of so much journalistic commentary. Perhaps Louis Tussaud's had decided that a dress was more appropriate. Ellis was exposed and concealed in the Chamber of Horrors. But what was the horror? What Ellis had done or what had been done to her?

In the House of Commons Mr Price, the Labour Member for Westhoughton, was outraged on behalf of the British public who had been 'shocked and scandalised by the gross commercialism of showmen in Blackpool … degrading the good name of Britain in the eyes of many foreign visitors and also demoralising the young people who were taken into those exhibitions'. Mr Price seemed to think that it was the effigy, rather than the hanging, that would corrupt the young and bring Britain into disrepute. He called on the Home Secretary to introduce legislation to ban such effigies. Gwilym Lloyd-George brushed aside his protests with libertarian disdain: 'It is not practicable, if indeed desirable, for every departure from good taste to be made subject to legislation.' Perhaps he was right – after all, the Ellis effigy was part of a long tradition in a country where public hanging had been more popular than any spectator sport; in 1807 45,000 people had crowded into the Newgate area to witness a double hanging and twenty-seven spectators were killed in the crush.

The execution of a woman was particularly troubling and troublesome for the Government; between 1900 and 1950, 130 were sentenced to death for murder in England and Wales but only twelve were executed. During the same period 1,080 men were sentenced to death for murder and 621 were executed. In 1953 the Report of the Royal Commission on Capital Punishment described a 'natural reluctance to carry out the death sentence on a woman'. Natural or not, governments were reluctant because it was unpopular with the press and it was ammunition for the abolitionist cause. Every time a woman was executed questions were asked about whether capital punishment as a whole was morally or socially acceptable.

The execution of Ellis dominated the front pages on 14 July and the story ran for weeks. It was an embarrassment to the Government and it was a great excuse for sensational revelations. Everyone sold their story: prison officers, hostesses, drinkers, racing car drivers, gamblers, each of them claiming to have had some unlikely encounter with Ellis that gave them a unique insight into her tragic fall. Television was becoming increasingly powerful – in 1953 20 million people (56 per cent of the adult population of Great Britain) had watched the

Coronation of Elizabeth II – and the Pathe News report of the execution was quick to turn the execution of Ellis into a historic moment. The footage of the crowd scenes outside Holloway were set to a sweeping orchestral score, building to a portentous crescendo behind the voice of the news, brimful with gravitas and urgency:

> For the hundreds who waited at Holloway gaol on the execution morning and for the millions who stayed away, three questions remain: Should a woman hang? Should anyone hang at all? Or should there be degrees of murder? Millions are asking, is it civilised to kill by law, does it really act as a deterrent, is it right to ask any human being to carry out the killing and if the law says that it is, should it be set aside merely because the murderer is a woman? This was the law of the centuries gone by, should it remain the law of the twentieth century?

The Government received hundreds of letters, condemning and supporting the execution with equal passion. Mrs Spoczynska of Maida Vale was anxious to express her admiration for the Home Secretary's 'courage and devotion to duty':

> As a mother of two children, British by birth and descent and proud of it, and having dedicated my life to campaigning and writing to further the cause of our British Christian traditions of honourable family life and decent living, I wish to express my personal appreciation … The fate of this self-confessed openly immoral and shameless woman will, I feel, prove a

> deterrent to many who might otherwise have been tempted to let lust rule their lives. Such women are a menace to our national standards, and there is now one such less to corrupt others by her example.

Others were upset not just by Ellis herself, but also by the newspaper coverage and the campaign to reprieve her. Captain MacManus, writing from the United Service Club in Dublin, was also upset by the campaign for a reprieve and the behaviour of the newspapers:

> I am taking the liberty of writing to you personally to express my sincere appreciation of the quiet moral courage and proper firmness which you have displayed … in the face of this really scandalous outburst of organised mass hysteria. What is really shocking is the reckless and deliberate way in which certain wealthy newspapers beat up and then organise mass hysteria and thus increase their circulation by unbridled sensationalism, quite regardless of the public good or the welfare of the people, even of the individual concerned and her family.

Mr Stuart of Ilford wanted the Home Secretary to know what he had felt the night before the execution: 'I cannot describe coherently what I, who am not even a relative of Mrs Ellis, went through mentally and spiritually that night, except to say that it was sheer, agonising hell. Perhaps you were sound asleep, or, if awake, wondering whether the coroner would remember to whitewash his post-mortem report with the customary decorum.' Alf Wathney of the Royal Norwegian Navy was baffled by the decision not to grant a reprieve: 'It is so hard for the Norwegians to understand how such kind people as the British can retain the capital punishment and hang the condemned man or woman … hanging does not belong to a Christian nation. It is pagan.' Norway was one of many countries which were horrified by the execution. According to the *Melbourne Argus*, 'Hanging shames Britain in the eyes of the civilised world.' The French press were unable to understand how a crime of passion could be treated in this way, and the British Ambassador in Stockholm wrote a long dispatch to Harold Macmillan, describing the reaction in Sweden: 'The campaign in the press has been quite exceptionally violent – indeed, I can think of no issue since I arrived in March, 1954, which has given rise to comparable criticism of our policy or institutions … The writings of the more sensational newspapers in Great Britain on this subject cause particular repugnance in the Swedish mind.'

This was an important point, and one that was causing concern in Britain. The effect of the execution was hugely amplified by the voyeuristic and salacious stories in the papers and by the public's seemingly insatiable appetite for the stories. The execution of Ellis had taken place, literally, inside the prison walls, but the newspapers had revealed it, made it public in their own way. By 1955 concealment was no longer possible – hanging had been brought out into the open again.

The editor of *The Lancet* was alarmed:

> A father at Holloway prison gates lifted up his six-year-old daughter so that she could say she had seen the notice announcing the death of Mrs. Ellis. Children in a school near the prison are described by one of their teachers as being in a ferment … Our

> means of communication are nowadays so efficient that the same unwholesome excitement was shared by children up and down the country. When an incident becomes the news of the day, presented at twenty million breakfast tables, it becomes for the time an important part of our national life ... We gild the worst of crimes with publicity, and associate it with an act of communal violence: small wonder if the youngsters swallowing the poison find the idea of violence dangerously attractive.

The leader in the *Spectator* was more cynical: 'It is no longer a matter for surprise that Englishmen deplore bull-fighting but delight in hanging. Hanging has become the national sport.' The *Spectator* article went on to condemn Gwilym Lloyd-George and to criticise his performance in a parliamentary debate on capital punishment where he seemed to directly contradict the evidence given by the Home Office to the Royal Commission on Capital Punishment:

> The irresistible conclusion is that he had not taken the trouble to read the report of the Royal Commission. Is it really too much to ask that the Home Secretary should spend rather less time in the smoking room of the House of Commons and rather more time reading official documents? Men who go on hanging women who should not be hanged can hardly expect to be held in universal esteem.

This criticism, which seems positively restrained by the standards of contemporary journalism, caused outrage. Lloyd-

George was so affronted that he considered taking legal action against the *Spectator*. He wrote to his old friend and former Home Secretary David Maxwell Fyfe QC, now Viscount Kilmuir, to ask for his advice: 'It is one thing to say that the Home Secretary is incompetent: no one can complain about that; but it is another to say that he is incompetent because he spends his time in the smoking room and neglects his official duties, and acts under pressure from his advisers.'

Viscount Kilmuir was damning of the article – 'as low an exhibition of journalism as I have ever seen' – but he discouraged Lloyd-George from taking any action, mainly on the grounds that a court case would 'be used as an abolitionist field day' and would expose the workings of government to unwonted attention: 'Although I think that any Minister who does not go regularly to the smoking-room is not doing his job properly, and have always acted on this view, I do not think that it would be a good thing for the dignity of government that this should be canvassed.' Lloyd-George's outrage seems risible now, but in 1955 the media were far more restrained in their scrutiny of politicians and it was possible to talk about 'the dignity of government' without sounding ridiculous. From the Government's point of view, Viscount Kilmuir was undoubtedly right: the newspaper coverage of the Ellis case had already done enough damage to the dignity of the leading political players.

Arthur Koestler had been deeply troubled by the cases of Evans and Bentley, but the execution of Ruth Ellis drove him into a campaigning frenzy. In the same month that Ellis was executed he began writing an abolitionist polemic, *Reflections on Hanging*, and he also went to the publisher and abolitionist Victor Gollancz with the idea of setting up a national campaign for the abolition of capital punishment. Gollancz agreed and the national campaign was launched in August. Throughout the hot summer of 1955 Koestler was working frantically on his abolitionist book, with the help of Cynthia Jefferies, who had been his secretary and later became his third wife. Jefferies was struck by Koestler's passion for his subject:

> He was like somebody possessed and the subject was never far from his mind. If we went to a pub for a drink, he would start up a discussion with the publican ... All publicans were pro-hanging, which, of course, was just what Arthur was hoping for, and he would present a diabolically reasoned and objective case for abolition. Although he never managed to convert a single die-hard publican, he never gave up hope.

At the height of the heatwave Koestler began to dictate to Jefferies the section of the book that described in detail the physical effects of an execution and the possible consequences of a botched execution. When Koestler was five years old he had been taken to see a man called Dr Neubauer in Budapest. Nobody told him what was going to happen to him. He was put in the chair and his tonsils were removed without an anaesthetic. He wrote about this experience in his autobiography, recalling those moments 'of choking and vomiting blood ... of utter loneliness, abandoned by my parents, in the clutches of a hostile and malign power, filled me with a kind of cosmic terror ... It is not unlikely that my subsequent preoccupation with physical violence, terror, and torture derives partly from this experience, and that Dr Neubauer paved the way for my becoming a chronicler of the more repulsive aspects of our time.' Koestler's passion and his horror drove him on and he finished the first draft of *Reflections on Hanging* by October 1955. In his own memoirs, Koestler's friend George Mikes remembered this passion: 'The fight for abolition was the bitterest and most determined fight of his life. He was quite obsessed about the struggle. He kept talking of it – indeed, in those days he hardly talked of anything else.'

On 10 November 1955 Sydney Silverman was granted leave to introduce the Death Penalty (Abolition) Bill and on the same day the National Campaign for the Abolition of Capital Punishment held its first public meeting in Central Hall, Westminster. The hall was filled to its capacity and a collection raised nearly £1,000 in the first twenty minutes. The trial and execution of Ruth Ellis had exposed Pierrepoint and it had brought abolition a step closer, but this was not the end of the story. The trial had an afterlife that is still continuing: a whole generation has grown old opining about the Ellis trial.

*

In 1971 John Bickford went to the police and made a statement about his involvement in the Ellis case. In this statement he said that when he was preparing the case for trial he had asked Cussen where Ellis had got the gun. Cussen told him that he, Cussen, had given it to her. According to Bickford, Cussen said that on the afternoon of the murder he had oiled the gun, given it to Ellis and taken her to a wood for target practice before driving her to Hampstead. Bickford also told the police that Ellis had confirmed that Cussen's account was true but that she had instructed Bickford that she did not want any of it to come out at the trial. There are lots of theories about why Ellis might have kept Cussen out of it – because she wanted to die, because Cussen had promised to look after her son after her death in exchange for her silence (he didn't), because she had agreed to keep silent in return for his help with the gun – but no one knows the answer.

Bickford told the police that he had not revealed what Cussen had told him because he had believed that he was bound by the rules of client confidentiality and that in any event his professional judgement was that, far from helping Ellis's case, the evidence about Cussen and the gun would have damaged it even further by bringing in more evidence of premeditation. (Of course Cussen might have been charged not just as an accessory but as a principal and then the whole feeling of the case would have been radically different.) In 1977 Bickford repeated this account when he was interviewed by Peter Williams for a television documentary. He died shortly after the programme was broadcast. Cussen always denied the allegation.

Cussen moved to Australia in 1964 and in 1977 he was tracked down by Peter Williams. At that time Cussen was running a florist's shop in Perth, Western Australia. It was called Chez Fleur. I was familiar with the photographs of Cussen from the 1950s and I was curious to see how he had aged. There is one old photograph that shows just Cussen and Ellis, sitting at a table. They are in a restaurant or a club and the picture looks as if it has been cropped, as if the other people at the table have been cut out. Ellis is wearing a dark dress with a pale polka-dot collar and a large polka-dot bow beneath the collar. She seems to be carefully posed – leaning towards the camera and smiling directly at it, with her elbow resting on the table and a wine glass in her hand. Cussen is sitting next to Ellis and his head is turned towards her. She is only interested in the camera and he is only interested in her. He is wearing a check suit, his moustache is very thin and his ears are rather large. His eyes are very small and his lips are as thin as his moustache. The expression on his face could be described as a half smile or as a mildly lascivious, mildly proprietorial leer. He looks like a provincial bank manager who has just got lucky.

More than twenty years later, in Chez Fleur, Cussen was less ebullient. The florist's was not going well – worms in the carnations – and he looked rather glum. He was asked about Bickford's allegations and once again he denied everything. He was asked what he was doing on the evening of 12 April 1955 when Ellis shot David Blakely. He smiled and shrugged his shoulders: 'One wouldn't remember what one exactly did when one went home.'

There will never be any irrefutable proof that Cussen gave Ellis the gun, but John Bickford's statement to the police is very convincing. Cussen had no explanation for why John Bickford might have made it all up, so long after the event. Cussen never returned to England; he died in Australia in 1991.

Sir Frank Newsam, the man who advised Gwilym Lloyd-George on whether to grant a reprieve to Ellis, retired from his post at the Home Office in 1957 and died seven years later. In 1999 Philip Allen, who was Newsam's assistant at the time, was interviewed by the BBC. He was asked about the decision not to grant a reprieve in the Ellis case: 'You may say we came to the wrong conclusion. I don't know. Perhaps we did.' He also said this: 'I gradually became a convinced abolitionist, having dealt with a number of these cases. It didn't seem to me to be right that an individual life should be taken. But we had to operate on the basis of what the law was and the law said that the punishment for murder is death by hanging.'

In 2003 the Ellis case was heard for the first time by the Court of Appeal. The Court dismissed the appeal and made it clear that they considered it a waste of their time: 'On any view, Mrs. Ellis had committed a serious criminal offence … and the only issue was the precise crime of which she was guilty.' The Court of Appeal was annoyed because it had been asked to spend precious time on an old case while people were waiting in prison to have their appeals against conviction heard, people who might have already spent months or even years in prison for a crime they did not commit.

In 2005 Muriel Jakubait published a book about her sister. In it she claimed that the shooting of Blakely was a set-up, engineered by the intelligence services. Her theory was that Ellis and Blakely were both on the MI5 pay role in a lowly capacity. Since 1950 Ellis had been secretly gathering intelligence from the movers and shakers who drank in the clubs where she worked. Cussen also worked for the intelligence services, at a more senior level. Cussen decided that Ellis and Blakely knew too much, that they had information which might embarrass the Government, and so he set up Ellis to shoot Blakely, in order to silence both of them. It was not the shots fired from Ellis's gun that actually killed Blakely. Cussen, the expert, was hiding in the bushes and fired the fatal shots. The defence lawyers chose not to cross-examine Cussen adequately and the judge ensured a guilty verdict by virtue of his rulings on the law. Her sister was murdered by the Establishment.

My personal opinion is that Muriel Jakubait's theory is absurd, but I think that she is describing a genuine sense of betrayal. The Ellis case and its aftermath is not about spies hiding in bushes, but it *is* about class and the workings of the class system in England in the 1950s. Trial by jury was, and still is, despite the efforts of the current administration, a system that genuinely protects the fundamental right to a fair trial. In 1955 the barristers and judges who were responsible for this system were almost all men with a public school education and a private income. This doesn't necessarily mean that Ellis's trial was less fair than it would be today, but it *does* mean that it was conducted in a very rarefied atmosphere. When Ellis was charged with murder she entered a world inhabited by people who spoke a different language and operated according to a different set of rules. They were acting according to the rules of the law and the rules of their own class. Two sets of rules, both of them inaccessible to Ellis, despite Bickford's efforts. It was a foreign country – the barristers and the judge had a guidebook but they weren't lending it to Ellis. I don't think it was a murderous conspiracy by MI5, it was simply the benign treachery of a system where the only people with the guidebook were the ones with an expensive education.

*

The Ellis case also had an afterlife in film: *Yield to the Night*, directed by J. Lee Thompson, was released in 1956, a year after the execution. The pre-title sequence follows a platinum blonde in stilettos whose face we never see. Silently, she journeys across London, gorgeous stockinged legs in and out of a black cab, crossing a strangely empty Trafalgar Square, the fountains brimming, before arriving at a mews house where she waits for the arrival of an expensive-looking brunette in furs and a convertible. At this point the blonde opens a smart clutch bag with gloved hands and removes a small revolver before shooting the brunette seven times in the back. Finally we see her face. It is Diana Dors.

In 1953, three years before *Yield to the Night* was released, J. Lee Thompson had directed Diana Dors in *The Weak and the Wicked*, a serious drama about women in prison. It was an unexpected casting: Dors was well known for her glitzy, scandalous lifestyle, the lifestyle Ellis would have liked – powder-blue Cadillacs, sequinned dresses and champagne – not for her acting abilities. Her most recent film had been a busty romp called *Is Your Honeymoon Really Necessary*?; a prison drama did not look like an obvious progression.

During the filming of *The Weak and the Wicked* Thompson discussed with Dors the possibility of playing the part of Mary Hilton, the condemned murderer in *Yield to the Night*, which was based on a book by Joan Henry. The film was shot in October 1955, six months after Ellis was executed, and it was released in the summer of 1956, just as the Abolition Bill was going through Parliament. The abolitionists used the film to publicise their campaign and Associated British Pictures used the execution of Ellis to publicise their film.

On the day that the Abolition Bill was scheduled for debate in the House of Lords the abolitionists arranged a special screening of *Yield to the Night* for their lordships at the National Film Theatre. (Only six of them turned up.) Associated British Pictures took the campaigning headlines from the Ellis case – 'Would you hang Ruth Ellis?' – and adapted them for their own purposes. Under a photograph of Dors, bare-shouldered, lips parted, very platinum, are these words: 'Would you hang Mary Hilton?' Ellis and Diana Dors were united again, only this time it was Ellis who had the top billing.

The British Board of Film Censors gave *Yield to the Night* an 'X' certificate, much to the annoyance of J. Lee Thompson: 'What the censors objected to was the whole premise, not any one particular scene – the torment of a woman in the death cell.' The *Daily Express* quoted a mother from Hove who spoke of the 'ghastliness of such films' and claimed that her nineteen-year-old daughter had been so affected by the film that after seeing it she had gassed herself. The film was a critical success but a box office failure. Perhaps the people who liked Diana Dors' movies were not interested in the capital punishment debate, or perhaps they disliked the message. There is no record of Diana Dors' views on capital punishment. In 1984 she wrote a book called *Diana Dors' A-Z of Men* and, under 'H is for Hangman', she gave an account of a meeting with Pierrepoint in 1953. Diana Dors was shocked – he was 'brash', with 'an ego bigger than any film star' – but she was 'drawn like a snake to a charmer' and he overwhelmed her with his gruesome revelations.

In *Yield to the Night* Mary Hilton is a charming young woman with a fabulous bosom who works on the perfume counter somewhere rather grand. Most of the film takes place in the condemned cell, and the events that led to the murder are told in flashback. Mary is married to Fred, whom she does not love. We gather that he is kind but dreary and does not appreciate her. Sadly for Mary, her brief encounter is not with Trevor Howard but a piano player called Jim, a handsome cad who is part Canadian (like Ellis's Locarno lover), and, like Blakely, has a liking for rich, classy women. Mary, who is neither rich nor classy, but entirely respectable, yet at the same time sexually confident and financially self-reliant, leaves her husband for the piano player. But she is too late: his heart has already been stolen by the rich brunette and although he and Mary enjoy some nice walks in the park together, we know it isn't going to last. Mary can't compete with the rich brunette: 'What do you think I am, a night club queen? I have to get up and do a day's work', and eventually she is left sobbing in her one-bedroom flat. Then the rich brunette dumps the piano player (class again) and, in a savage twist, he kills himself. It is up to Mary to avenge his death. Fortunately the piano player left a small revolver in Mary's flat a few scenes earlier when he came back to her in desperation after the rich brunette refused to answer his calls. He had been planning to kill himself with the revolver, but Mary locked it in a drawer and talked him out of it. Now she takes the gun and the rest is history.

Despite a weak plot and a series of creaky clichés, it is a strange and effective melodrama. The heart of the film is in the condemned cell, where Mary waits for death, not knowing if she will be granted a reprieve. Mary refuses to conform. She rejects Fred, the doggedly loyal husband, and remains faithful to the piano player: 'I never loved anyone but Jim.' Like Ellis, and Diana Dors, she believes that she has bettered herself. She shudders at the accent and sentiment of her badly dressed mother: 'We must 'ave 'ope.' Unlike Ellis, she doesn't want to die: 'I know I've done wrong. It doesn't make me want to die.' As the days pass and Mary's roots darken, she gradually sinks into a kind of terrified inertia, drowning in slow motion, alone except for the kindly and brisk prison warders who feed her, bathe her, cut her nails and play chess with her. The message is hammered home in Mary's interior monologue: 'They have a funny look in their eyes, like I had once. For they're going to kill someone too. Only this time it's legal.' She is never left alone in the cell and the light in the cell is never turned off. The Governor tells her that there will be no reprieve and she will be executed in two days' time. The world of the condemned cell becomes increasingly surreal as Mary, who is not dying, moves temporally closer to death. Diana Dors' performance as a confused young woman who cannot make any sense of what is happening to her is bleak and very moving. At the end of the film Mary walks towards the camera, into darkness.

CHAPTER TWELVE

Abolition

'She had put on a dab of lipstick, but that was all. Even so, I was rather moved to see it. Most men condemned to death take the trouble to shave and comb their hair carefully. But Ruth Ellis's lipstick was a poignant reminder that she was still a woman, though in the condemned cell she had worn spectacles nearly all the time, and let her hair stray loose down her back.'

This is an extract from Pierrepoint's account of the execution of Ruth Ellis. Or rather, it is an account written in his name by an anonymous journalist. It was written in March 1956 for the *Empire News and Sunday Chronicle*. The Government threatened the newspaper and Pierrepoint with prosecution under the Official Secrets Act and the article was cut. Instead of a front-page scoop on the secrets of the gallows, the newspaper carried a front-page story about government censorship: 'RUTH ELLIS HOME OFFICE GAG. PIERREPOINT TOLD: YOU MAY NOT REVEAL HER LAST WORDS.' Now the original, uncensored version of the article sits between brown covers in the National Archives in Kew.

A visit to Kew is always a treat, a day out. The train grinds through the endlessly grey reaches of north London – Gospel Oak, Brondesbury, Kensal Rise, Willesden Junction, Acton

Central. As it crosses the river it seems to enter another country, leafy suburbia bringing order out of chaos, and when I obediently alight at Kew Gardens ('Alight here for the National Archives') and follow the thoughtfully placed signs, I always feel as if Mary Poppins and Bert are just around the corner, waiting to take me by the hand. The building is ugly, but it has a lake, with swans and rustling bamboo, and there are dozens of benches. So much landscaping, so much civic energy devoted to looking after me, a member of the public; I am touched and even flattered, coming from a part of London where the only bench is strictly reserved for the local drunks. By the time I have settled down in the archive itself and gently removed the frayed white ribbon that holds together the covers of my first file, I am almost overcome with excitement and gratitude. Millions of records and documents, saved and cherished for hundreds of years. Anyone can look at them, and it is absolutely and completely free. My sentimental moments at the National Archive are the nearest I get to patriotic feeling.

But the day I found the Ruth Ellis article was different. I was looking for something else and I came upon it by accident. I read the first paragraph and felt sick. I wanted to shut the file, pack my bag and leave the building. I wanted to stop spying on dead people, to pick myself up out of the gutter, read poetry, cook, clear my mind. I also wanted to read the article. Perhaps I was just a grubby voyeur, free to indulge my basest instincts thanks to the passage of time, no longer protected from myself by the nanny state. Or perhaps I was guided by higher principles, in search of the historical truth. I read the article. Then I made a note of it. The reader is made to wait for four pages before the moment comes:

> I put my arm around her shoulder, and said: 'Come with me, luv, I'm not going to hurt you.' I didn't walk in front of her, saying 'Follow me', as I usually do with a man. I led her in, and she walked with me utterly calmly, nor did she flinch at the sight of the apparatus of execution. I lifted up her long, loosely-combed fair hair, but I did it so quickly that I'm not sure if she really felt what I was doing with her hair, for she had glimpsed the white cap in my other hand, over her head, and pouted again. 'Have I got to have that thing on?' I said: 'Yes, luv, I'm sorry,' but I doubt very much if she heard me finish the sentence, for she was already gone before I'd done speaking. And that was how I intended it.

I left the notes alone for a long time, but I knew that I would have to come back to them eventually. The article itself, probably more fiction than fact, was simply nasty, but I wanted to understand how it was that Pierrepoint, the most discreet and reliable of public servants, had agreed that it should be published in his name and had then been threatened with prosecution by the Government. This was the man on whom the Government had bestowed the rank of Lieutenant-Colonel in order to fly him to Germany, Austria, Egypt and Gibraltar to demonstrate the British way of hanging. They had entrusted to him the execution of the most infamous Nazi war criminals and British traitors. He had always carried out his official duties in an exemplary fashion. He was the only public executioner ever to be called to give evidence before a Royal Commission. In his autobiography Pierrepoint described his work as a sacred duty which set him apart from his fellow men. It was his calling. By

1956, after more than 400 perfect executions, he might have been expecting to see his name on a list of birthday honours, not on a notice of prosecution. What went wrong?

On 2 January 1956 Pierrepoint left the Rose and Crown pub in Hoole, near Preston, and travelled to Manchester to prepare for the execution of Thomas Bancroft, scheduled for the following day. A reprieve was usually granted several days before the execution date, so by 2 January it seemed likely that Bancroft's execution would go ahead. Pierrepoint had hired temporary bar staff to cover for him so that business would not suffer in his absence. Very late in the day, after Pierrepoint had calculated the drop and prepared the gallows, Bancroft received a reprieve. Pierrepoint left the prison at about 8.30 in the evening and the snow prevented him from returning to Hoole until the following morning. Then, as usual, he waited for his payment from the County Sheriff. Pierrepoint was a freelance and although the Prison Commissioners were responsible for appointing executioners and compiling the list of approved executioners, the County Sheriffs paid them for each job.

A couple of weeks later he received a letter from the Under-Sheriff of Lancashire. It contained his travelling expenses but no execution fee. Pierrepoint immediately went above the head of the Sheriff and on 25 January he wrote to the Prison Commissioners to complain that this was unfair because he had spent time away from his pub and incurred the cost of taking on extra staff. He claimed that on other occasions he had received the full fee when there was a reprieve, and he asked them to reconsider his payment. (There was no national pay scale for executioners and the amount was at the discretion of individual Sheriffs. It is not clear whether there was a standard amount for reprieves, but it certainly was *not* standard practice to pay the full fee. If Pierrepoint really had been paid a full fee for another reprieve it may have been a measure of his status as Number One, or it may have been a postcode lottery.)

The Prison Commissioners replied two weeks later, passing the buck straight back to the Sheriff: 'This matter rests between the executioner and the Sheriff concerned.' Pierrepoint didn't reply to this letter for some time. The letter had arrived in Hoole at the beginning of February, just days after the Leader of the House of Commons had announced that the long-awaited debate on capital punishment would take place within three weeks and that there would be a free vote. Perhaps Pierrepoint was wise to wait.

Eden's government was in favour of the death penalty, but there was to be a free vote in the Commons and the outcome was uncertain. The climate of opinion was changing: the membership of the National Campaign for the Abolition of Capital Punishment had reached nearly 33,000 and they were vigorously lobbying MPs. The *Observer*, the *Spectator* and *Picture Post* were all campaigning for abolition and the serialisation of Koestler's *Reflections on Hanging* in the *Observer* was attracting a lot of attention. Just as Koestler had hoped, it caused outrage amongst the legal establishment. The book opens with a wonderful commentary on the 'peaceful country' where necks are broken:

> There seems to be a jolliness about the procedure as if the victim twitching at the end of the rope were not a real person but a dummy burnt on Guy Fawkes' Day … The present hangman, Pierrepoint, runs a public house called *Help the Poor Struggler* … and the present Lord Chief Justice delighted a Royal Academy

> banquet with a story of a judge who, after passing the death sentence on three men, was welcomed by a band playing the Eton Boating Song's refrain: 'We'll all swing together' … It all goes to show that hanging has a kind of macabre cosiness, like a slightly off-colour family joke, which only foreigners, abolitionists and other humourless creatures are unable to share.

On 16 February 1956 the Home Secretary, Gwilym Lloyd-George, opened the Commons debate by declaring that nobody had ever been hanged as a result of a wrongful conviction. He was challenged by George Rogers MP, an abolitionist who had campaigned for a reprieve for Ruth Ellis: 'Mark these words, Mr Speaker: I will make the Home Secretary eat those words before I am much older … I will demonstrate that Evans was innocent and the judges were wrong.' (In fact George Rogers was ten years older when Evans was granted a posthumous free pardon in 1966. Gwilym Lloyd-George died the following year.) George Rogers also reminded the Home Secretary of the wider consequences of the death penalty: 'Ruth Ellis had a son. I took that boy into my house to try and save him from the horror of the day of execution. Can you imagine the agony experienced by my wife and children when they had to pretend to that fatherless boy that everything was normal when at the same time his mother was being taken from the condemned cell to be hanged?'

Sydney Silverman also spoke, and concluded his speech in favour of abolition with rousing rhetoric: 'Let us as free men, free women, free members of Parliament in a free society, go forward and wipe this dark stain from our statute book forever.'

The Government was defeated by a majority of thirty-one. Koestler was in the Visitors' Gallery and recorded the debate in his diary: '*Unforgettable* … Incredible surprise vote.' The following day The *Times* announced: 'Commons to End Death Penalty.' The abolitionists had won the first round, but there were more to come. Last, but not least, there was the House of Lords.

Six days later, on 23 February, Pierrepoint replied to the Prison Commissioners. In addition to his travelling expenses, he had now received £4 from the Under-Sheriff:

> I must inform you that I was extremely dissatisfied with this payment, and now I regard this kind of meaness [*sic*] as surprising in view of my experience and long service. In the circumstances I have made up my mind to resign and this letter must be accepted as a letter of resignation. I request the removal of my name from the list of executioners forthwith.

It was a bombshell, and it left the Prison Commissioners and the Home Office in a very tight spot; none of the other executioners on the list had ever carried out an execution, they had only acted as assistants to Pierrepoint. Politically, it was a bad moment for the Government to be seen to be in a muddle over executioners. They were faced with a potentially disastrous combination: a press with an insatiable appetite for gruesome stories of the gallows, an abolitionist movement that was gaining increasing support and publicity, and an ex-hangman with a grievance and a good sense of timing.

The press knew about Pierrepoint's resignation before the Home Office; Pierrepoint's letter of resignation was written on a Thursday and the newspapers carried the story the following day, pre-empting a gently understated memo from the Prison Commissioners to Sir Frank Newsam, the Permanent Under-Secretary of State at the Home Office, to inform him of the resignation and warn him that 'there may be some publicity'. In fact, there was a great deal of publicity: The *Sunday Times* put the resignation on the front page and claimed that it had nothing to do with the vote on capital punishment; the *Sunday Pictorial* agreed that it was unconnected to the vote and claimed that Pierrepoint had been considering resigning for some time. By Monday the papers were looking for more zest in the story and the *Daily Sketch* headline was: 'Ruth Ellis decided Pierrepoint', while the *Daily Express* had Pierrepoint, man of mystery: 'Now Pierrepoint Slips Abroad ... He left on Saturday, with his wife. And no one quite knows where they have gone. Not even their 19-year-old daughter Freda. Pierrepoint always moved mysteriously. He rarely left forwarding addresses.'

Pierrepoint didn't slip abroad and he didn't have a daughter, but after sending his letter of resignation he and Anne did go on holiday to France. While they were away Sir Frank spoke to a Mr Russell at the Prison Commissioners' office and told him to get Pierrepoint back to work. Clearly the Home Office needed Pierrepoint in the fold, not bleating outside. So the Sheriff of Lancashire was made to pay the full fee of £15 for the cancelled execution and on the morning of 29 February Mr Russell sent a weasel-worded letter to Pierrepoint: 'I understand that he [the Sheriff] has now been authorised to pay you the difference ... Would you be good enough to let me know, as a matter of urgency, whether you still wish your name to be removed from the list?'

Hopefully Pierrepoint would take the money and see sense

and Sir Frank would be satisfied. But it was not to be; later the same day, after the letter had been sent to Pierrepoint, Mr Russell received an internal memo with more disturbing news:

> Miss Nunn rang with some 'grapevine' information. A friend of hers in F.2 lunched the other day with an acquaintance of his who happened to be the Feature Editor of the *Sunday Dispatch*. This journalist said quite categorically he knew that Pierrepoint's memoirs were already written and that he had been offered between £30,000 and £40,000 by the *Empire News* for their publication. One wonders whether he is doing the 'Grand Tour' on the proceeds of the first instalment!

Mr Russell, on a salary of £2,000 a year, may well have wondered, but he rose above the sordid financial details and wrote again to Pierrepoint, reminding him, quite politely, of the legal position:

> The Commissioners appreciate that your conduct in the past has given them every ground for confidence in your discretion, but in order to prevent the possibility of any misunderstanding I venture to remind you on their behalf that in pursuance of the Official Secrets Acts, 1911 and 1920, you would require their authority before disclosing any information obtained in your official capacity, and that this requirement would still operate if you ceased to act as an executioner.

The next day the front page of *Empire News* and the *Sunday Chronicle* cleared up any misunderstanding: 'Albert Pierrepoint is to tell the story of his amazing life and experiences ... Next Sunday you will meet – PIERREPOINT: THE MAN.' Curiously, for a paper that was not known for its political or social agenda, *Empire News* was anxious to remind its readers that there was a higher purpose to buying next week's edition: 'He hanged Haigh, the acid bath killer, Heath, the sex maniac, Christie ... Ruth Ellis ... Bentley ... The traitor, William Joyce ... BUT HIS STORY IS MORE THAN A PROCESSION OF THE CONDEMNED. IT IS NO MERE HANGMAN'S DIARY. It is a social document of immediate importance and public interest.' The story was accompanied by a large photograph of Pierrepoint and his wife. Anne is wearing a fur coat and her lips are parted in a grimace. Pierrepoint's smile is reassuringly in place and he seems to be trying out a semi-professional twinkle. The caption reads: 'Cigar in hand, Albert Pierrepoint steps out with his blonde wife Anne at the start of a Riviera holiday.' Anne looks rather dignified. Photographed on her own she might be mistaken for a head-teacher, leading a delegation to a cold place where a fur coat would be rather sensible; standing beside Pierrepoint the coat seems an obviously poor choice for the Riviera. Mrs Pierrepoint was not well cast as the hangman's moll.

Clearly Pierrepoint had struck a deal with *Empire News* before he wrote his letter of resignation and left for the Riviera, but the timing of that deal is unclear. According to a contemporary article in the *World's Press News*, Pierrepoint had spent the last three years speaking to two journalists who were preparing his memoirs. They ran to 50,000 words and were sold to *Empire News* for somewhere in the region of £40,000. If this is true, it is rather shocking; it means that three years after giving evidence before the Royal Commission Pierrepoint had broken his own rules, betraying the vow of silence that he had made to himself, no longer 'a man apart' but a celebrity in the making, waiting to spill the beans at the right moment and buy himself a pension. His silence had become a precious commodity. The execution of Ruth Ellis in 1955 and the parliamentary vote to abolish capital punishment in 1956 may not have driven Pierrepoint to resign, but they did increase the value of his life story.

On his return from France Pierrepoint replied to Mr Russell, thanking him for his 'kind sentiments' and protesting that if he had been paid the full fee by the Sheriff of Lancashire in the first place, he would not have resigned:

> Now, however, so much has been printed about the supposed reasons for my resignation, including the alleged effect on me of the execution of Ruth Ellis, that I find in fairness to myself, I must make the position clear in the public mind.
>
> It is true that I have entered into an arrangement for this reason for the publication of a series of artickles [*sic*] about my career, but I can assure you that the discretion, to which you were kind enough to refer in your letter of March 3, will be exercised in this respect also. Substantially, I shall not go beyond what has already been published including the evidence given before the Royal Commission on Capital Punishment, and what Sir Gowers has said in his arickles [*sic*].
>
> Naturally, I have had experiences which would cause considerable controversy but these are locked in my heart, and I am never going to divulge them.

> I am afraid that I must keep my decision to ask for my name to be removed from the list of executioners, although I am aware that the other persons on the list may not be capable of carrying out an execution to the satisfaction of all concerned.

It is hard not to be put off by Pierrepoint's pious tone and his absurdly self-righteous justification for selling his story to the papers. If he had only wanted to 'make the position clear in the public mind', he could have delayed his holiday and made a statement to the press. What about the 'experiences which would cause considerable controversy', safely locked away in Pierrepoint's heart? Is this a veiled threat or a genuine declaration of good faith? Is his reference to his evidence to the Royal Commission a pertinent reminder to Mr Russell of the difficulties of invoking the Official Secrets legislation or an expression of his own enduring sense of betrayal and exposure?

Pierrepoint had grown up, both personally and professionally, with newspaper accounts of the reminiscences of his own father, John Ellis and countless other hangmen, and he understood the economic necessity of creating a public image for his retirement. But he also took great pride in his work. It was the thing that set him apart from, and above, his peers. This wasn't just about money. The final sentence of Pierrepoint's letter to Mr Russell is fraught with ambivalence: 'If, however, an occasion should arise in the future on which you think my services are necessary, I should be prepared to consider an individual case.' The mask of pious regret is suddenly stripped away. What did Pierrepoint want? Was it one last performance, for a specially invited audience? Was it the need to know that his status would endure, that he really was the best in the business?

Pierrepoint's hypocritical piety was a smart response to Mr Russell's invocation of the Official Secrets Acts; the correspondence between these two men was really a polite exchange of half-truths and threats, wrapped up in the language of sentiment, discretion and courtesy. The liberal state, which depended on the idea of voluntary restraint, had come face to face with its own Caliban and undoubtedly both sides were being economical with the truth. Russell knew that Pierrepoint was following in a long tradition; for more than half a century ex-hangmen had been publishing their memoirs and it is unsurprising that Pierrepoint's declaration of discretion did not entirely convince him. He wrote again to Pierrepoint, suggesting that 'it would be best if you would let [the Commissioners] see the script before publication.' Pierrepoint replied on 14 March 1956, agreeing to this proposal, and the following day Silverman's Abolition Bill was read for a second time and carried by a majority of twenty-four.

The first article was not troublesome. It set the scene, describing the origins of Pierrepoint's childhood ambition to follow in the footsteps of his father and uncle. The Commission suggested a couple of minor changes and the editor of *Empire News* complied. The story was illustrated by two large photographs of Pierrepoint looking jovial in his pub, surrounded by smiling men in suits. One of the captions reads: 'Intent faces ring the bar of the Rose and Crown Inn … as landlord Albert Pierrepoint plays "find the thimble" with his customers.' The Commission treated the article like an unpleasant smell: 'It was, of course, deplorable that a paper should pander to the morbid tastes of the public by publishing an article by a former executioner at all, but in this article, rubbishy as it was, there was nothing to which official objection could be taken.'

On the morning of Friday 23 March the Commissioners

received the next article. It contained detailed descriptions of the executions of Christie and Evans and it was going to be published on Sunday 25 March. There were no real revelations but it was spiced up with descriptions of intimate moments on the scaffold and a declaration of Pierrepoint's own unshakeable belief in the guilt of both men. That afternoon the Commission visited the offices of *Empire News* and demanded that the editor remove particular passages from the article. He refused. He was warned that if it was published in full Pierrepoint would be liable to prosecution under the Official Secrets Acts. The editor refused to back down: during the debate on amendments to the Official Secrets Act in 1920 the Attorney General had repeatedly reassured Parliament that the act could not be used to censor the press and now the Government was threatening to do precisely that. On Friday morning *Empire News* had one sensational story; on Friday evening they had two.

The paper ran the 'uncensored' Christie and Evans story on pages two and three and the censorship story on the front page: 'Home Office Try To Gag Pierrepoint.' The front page was devoted to a detailed account of the Commission's attempts to prevent publication and what purported to be Pierrepoint's own response to the Government's threat:

> It is surely in the public interest that the facts should be known, especially at this time when the death penalty is being debated in Parliament … I do not understand why it should even be contemplated that the Official Secrets Act should be used to suppress information which the public has a right to know. There is nothing in my article which could possibly be said to affect the safety of this country.

Pierrepoint, sounding entirely unlike himself, had suddenly become a champion of democratic debate and press freedom. It was a coup for *Empire News*, a severe embarrassment for Mr Russell and the Prison Commission, and a political disaster for the Government. A prosecution, successful or not, would be a political minefield and would provide the abolitionists with endless ammunition. A failure to prosecute would be a humiliating climb-down and a triumph for the press. *Empire News* had succeeded in backing the Government into a corner: damned if they prosecuted, damned if they didn't. But where did this leave Pierrepoint?

The Christie/Evans story was published on 25 March. On 27 March two men met for a drink in the Red Lion in Whitehall. It was lunchtime but they didn't eat anything. On leaving, one headed towards Kemsley House, the home of *Empire News*. The other man returned to New Scotland Yard. The men were Pierrepoint and Detective Superintendent Edmund Daws, the man who had arranged a police escort to get Pierrepoint into prison to execute Derek Bentley. In itself, the fact that Pierrepoint was drinking with a police officer was not surprising. The police were his friends; they drank in his pub and helped him out when he was in a tight spot. Tommy Mann says that the police appreciated Pierrepoint: 'He was the man who did the final job.' Prison officers held him in the same high regard and every Christmas throughout the 1960s and 1970s Tommy drove Pierrepoint to Strangeways prison for the carol service: 'He was a celebrity there.'

It is not clear who set up the meeting on the 27 March, but it came at an extremely sensitive moment for both men: Daws was a senior member of the CID at New Scotland Yard, and just yards from the Red Lion the question of whether or not to prosecute Pierrepoint was the subject of discussions between the Under-Secretary of State at the Home Office, the Attorney General and the Director of Public Prosecutions. The discussion that took place between the two men was recorded in a formal statement, made by Daws two days after the meeting. Daws' statement was part of the written evidence enclosed with the brief sent on behalf of the Director of Public Prosecutions, seeking advice from counsel on whether there should be a prosecution in relation to the article published on 25 March.

According to Daws' statement, it was Pierrepoint who suggested that they should meet. He told Daws that he had decided to sell his story because he was grossly insulted by the reprieve incident and had decided that 'there is no sentiment in business'. He appeared not to have heard of the Official Secrets Acts and said that the paper had 'promised they will look after me in the event of trouble'. Daws is worried that his old friend is being mercilessly exploited: 'In my view, the paper had no interest in him personally, all they were after was a scoop.' Daws goes on to say that Pierrepoint confided in him: 'You know if I was to tell you all I know I could kill capital punishment', whereupon Daws told him not to be such a fool and to remember the Official Secrets Acts. (What on earth was Pierrepoint hinting at? The incompetence of his fellow hangmen, leading to appallingly botched executions, perhaps? He cannot have been alluding to his own experiences, because he didn't make mistakes.) Daws ends his account of the meeting with this observation: 'I formed the impression that Pierrepoint, who, as I have said, I have known for fifteen years, is just an ordinary simple individual who had been misled by the press.'

Daws goes on to say that on his return to New Scotland Yard he spoke to Detective Chief Superintendent Kennedy, who was in charge of the investigation into the articles, and then tried to get hold of Pierrepoint to warn him of an important development. He concludes the statement by explaining why he has made it: 'This was a conversation between friends of long standing and I was not seeking to get information for the purposes of a prosecution, and this statement is submitted for guidance should a prosecution ensue and efforts be made by the legal advisor to the press to exploit this meeting between Pierrepoint and myself.'

The fact that this statement exists at all is really extraordinary. If the contents of the statement were true, it reveals great loyalty on Daws' part. In the knowledge that Pierrepoint may have committed a criminal offence, Daws was prepared not only to advise his old friend, but also to pass on to him confidential information about the criminal investigation. What motivated him? Friendship, perhaps, or a shared antipathy to the men in Whitehall and Westminster whose political lives depended upon the dirty work of those whose hands they must never be seen to shake. Having leaked information to his friend, Daws must then have realised that *Empire News* had got wind of it, perhaps because Pierrepoint was, as he says, such a 'simple individual'. So he alerted his superior officer and made a written statement describing details of his own leak within highly sensitive criminal proceedings, to ensure that the newspaper's lawyers would not be able to suggest that he was attempting to get information out of Pierrepoint in an unorthodox way.

The meeting between Pierrepoint and Daws was not the only significant event on 27 March. A quarter of a mile away, at the Royal Courts of Justice, the Attorney General was writing to the Prime Minister: 'I think I should inform you that a prosecution may shortly be instituted under the Official Secrets Act … It is all very tiresome. Enquiries into the matter are not yet completed but I think I shall have to give my consent to the prosecution … I am writing to inform you of the situation as I feel you would like to know it.'

The impending prosecution had the makings of a serious political setback for the Government. The newspapers would campaign against it on the grounds that it was an attempt to use the Official Secrets Acts for censorship. The abolitionists would seize on it as evidence that the Government had something to hide, which could only be bad; if capital punishment was really a just and humane form of punishment, there would be no reason to hide any aspect of it from the public. The trial itself could reveal cupboards packed with the skeletons of administrative incompetence and political hypocrisy, quite apart from a store of gruesome stories from the gallows. In other words, it was tiresome.

On 28 March, the day after his meeting with Daws in the Red Lion, Pierrepoint had another meeting with a senior police officer. But this time it was not in a pub. It was at Kemsley House, in the presence of a solicitor. Kemsley House was an imposing place, the headquarters of one of the great press barons of the time, Lord Kemsley. He was a self-made man and a self-styled anachronism, chauffeured everywhere in a high-bodied Rolls Royce, dressed in a black coat and striped trousers, with a black silk tie and a pearl tiepin. The lifts at Kemsley House always had to be opened five minutes before Lord Kemsley's arrival and the atmosphere in the offices was compared to that of a medieval court.

Lord Kemsley was out of the country on 28 March, so he could not object to the presence of a police officer in his kingdom. Superintendent Kennedy had come to Kemsley House to interview Pierrepoint and Mr Grafton Green, the editor of *Empire News:* 'I introduced myself and indicated that … in the first place I would like to speak to Mr Pierrepoint alone. I said to Pierrepoint, "Have you any objection?" and then he said, "I'll take what Mr Grafton Green says." ' The newspaper's solicitor intervened and reminded Kennedy that he would be present during the interview. Pierrepoint was then formally cautioned: 'This interview is being conducted at the request of the Director of Public Prosecutions in pursuance of enquiries into offences under the Official Secrets Acts.' Acting on legal advice, Pierrepoint made no comment. Kennedy concluded the interview in this way: 'I am not the person to decide what action may be taken but I do suggest that you should seriously consider your position before any further articles of a nature of last Sunday's should be published.' When Pierrepoint left Kemsley House that evening he may have reflected on Kennedy's words. And he may have felt that he was being bullied, quietly.

On 29 March, the day after Pierrepoint was interviewed by Kennedy, Daws made his formal statement. On the same day the editor of *Empire News* wrote to Mr Russell about Pierrepoint's next article, due to be published on 1 April. It was about the execution of Ruth Ellis. Mr Russell wanted cuts. The editor was outraged – 'I consider it is quite unreasonable' – but, on this occasion, he made the cuts: 'In view of all the circumstances, however, I am deleting [the relevant passages] from the article.' If the editor had also been quietly bullied by Detective Chief Superintendent Kennedy, it didn't stop him scoring a point the following Sunday. If he couldn't print the lurid details about Ruth Ellis, he could at least print the lurid details of his battle with Mr Russell. At the top of the story there was a photograph of Ruth Ellis, holding a wine glass and smiling. At the bottom was a photograph of Gwilym Lloyd-George, looking glum. The censored article that was printed in the *Empire News* contains none of the prurient detail that had made me feel so sick in the National Archives. The description of Ruth Ellis's last moments reads more like a sermon than a scoop: 'In her last moments I was as gentle as I could possibly be with Ruth Ellis. She was paying her price but it was a time for pity not for mistaken sympathy, and the performing of this sad task certainly did not upset me as people have tried to make out. Ruth Ellis died instantly, quicker even than the man she killed.'

While Mr Russell was politely reminding the editor of *Empire News* that he was going to end up in the dock, a public relations officer was drafting a confidential memo to Sir Frank Newsam, politely reminding him of the pros (there weren't any) and cons (numerous) of a prosecution. The main concern was how to put a positive spin on the reasons why the Government had wanted to prevent publication in the first place:

> I would like to suggest that a good administrative reason should be given, rather than public decency and good taste. The latter would be likely to provoke some Editors and MPs to challenge the right of the Home Secretary to be an arbiter of good taste, and to use the Official Secrets Act for that purpose. If, on the other hand, a good case were made on the narrower grounds of staff discipline, for example, or the Commissioners' responsibilities to prisoners and their relatives, it would be difficult for the press not to accept it as being within the Commissioners' competence. No doubt

> the Prison Commissioners do have reasons of this kind and would have no difficulty in stating them convincingly.

The reference to 'staff discipline' is slightly opaque, but the suggestion seems to be that if prison staff read about executions, they would be so unnerved that they would not be able to carry out their duties properly. Or that they might rise up in protest. It is a smokescreen, allowing the Government to avoid giving a true explanation of their motives.

In 1956 the British Government understood that capital punishment was only a useful tool for the state if it was represented in a way that was useful to the state. The deterrent justification for capital punishment is that the significance of an execution is not so much in the act itself but rather in the effect that it has on others. Deterrence ceases to operate so efficiently if the state loses control over the nature of the representation of the execution. By 1956 the tension between the need to represent the execution and the need to control the nature of that representation was becoming very difficult for the Government to manage. The post-war electorate was demanding more open government and greater accountability, and already the Royal Commission had published shocking details about the execution process. The Government did not want the public to know any more, but they could not afford to be seen to be pulling the strings. It was the era of public relations.

Three days after the publication of the censored Ruth Ellis story, the Director of Public Prosecutions received counsel's opinion on whether Pierrepoint should be prosecuted under the Official Secrets Acts. Maxwell Turner QC did not believe that there were grounds for a prosecution. Firstly, Mr Russell had made a mistake in asking Pierrepoint to send him the script of each article, because this meant that Pierrepoint was entitled to assume that whatever was published had been authorised by the Prison Commissioners. Secondly, the articles were not actually written by Pierrepoint but by journalists, who had embellished and exaggerated. The Official Secrets Acts were designed to prevent the communication of information. If the information turned out to be fiction, the prosecution would fail.

There was an interlude of about two weeks while everyone digested this opinion. Not everyone agreed with it. Sir Frank Newsam wrote to the Director of Public Prosecutions, reassuring him that 'the Home Office would not wish to make any representations in favour of or against prosecution in this case' and enclosing four and a half closely typed pages setting out the reasons why he disagreed with Maxwell Turner's advice. But on 18 April the Attorney General advised the Home Secretary, 'I have, not without some regret, come to the conclusion that I cannot issue my fiat for a prosecution.'

It was over. Fiction had triumphed over fact and hanging was still a spectacle. Pierrepoint did not find himself in the dock at the Old Bailey, but nor did he find himself in print for very much longer. On his return to England, Lord Kemsley immediately sent the Home Secretary a polite note, asking to see him as soon as possible. The two men met on 11 April 1956 and the Home Secretary made a brief handwritten note of their meeting. In inverted commas Lloyd George recorded this: 'Should he cancel the lot?' After the Ruth Ellis article there were a couple more instalments and then, in any event, the whole series was quietly dropped. Voluntary restraint was still alive and kicking, at least amongst the upper echelons of the Establishment.

Pierrepoint returned to the Rose and Crown in Hoole.

Blackboard Jungle was released and Teddy boys went wild for Bill Hayley's 'Rock Around the Clock', ripping up seats and dancing in the cinemas. The *Preston Guardian* announced that it was quite happy with the new independent television channel: 'The great virtue of ITV is that it gives us somewhere else to turn.' In July 1956 the Egyptian leader Gamal Abdel Nasser nationalised the Suez Canal Company, which had been jointly owned by Britain and France. The canal was a historic trade route for Britain and the main route for the oil on which the British economy depended. The response of the British Government was a test of Britain's international standing and it was a catastrophic failure. In October 1956, the month in which the Soviet Union brutally suppressed the Hungarian uprising, the British and the French colluded with Israel's attack on Egypt. The United States quickly forced a humiliating withdrawal: Eden's political career was finished and Britain could no longer consider itself a world power. The fierce domestic opposition to Eden's policy marked a sea-change in the political culture of Britain. The BBC was criticised by the Conservative Party for its lack of loyalty in its coverage of the Suez crisis and middle-class liberal opinion turned against the Conservatives. The post-Coronation idea of a new Elizabethan age was exposed as a fiction and ridiculed by John Osborne in *Look Back in Anger*.

Amidst the disintegration of a certain kind of national identity, the House of Commons continued to debate the death penalty. Conservative MPs were frantically tabling amendments to the Death Penalty (Abolition) Bill with the aim of weakening or wrecking it. They failed. On 28 June the Abolition Bill had its third reading and once again the Government was defeated. The Bill was passed by a majority of nineteen. But the real hurdle was yet to come: the House of Lords.

In 1948 the Commons had voted in favour of suspending the death penalty for five years and the Lords had voted against it by an overwhelming majority. Koestler understood the threat that the Lords posed to the abolitionist cause and he had always been cautious about the significance of the Commons vote in favour of abolition. In July 1956, as Nasser took control of the Suez Canal, the Lords debated the Abolition Bill. The Lord Chancellor, Lord Kilmuir, who as Home Secretary had refused to grant a reprieve to Derek Bentley, called on the House to reject the bill. In his memoirs he recalled the drama of the occasion: 'It was the greatest gathering of peers since 1945, and perhaps since 1914. The Chamber, the peeresses' box and the galleries were all packed, and, it being high summer, the ladies' dresses superimposed colour on the tension which always comes when strong and indeed violent views are held.' Almost as good as Ascot! The debate lasted two days and more than sixty peers spoke, including both Archbishops.

The Church was deeply divided on the issue. The Bishop of Winchester, who was in favour of retaining the death penalty, spoke of the sacrificial overtones of hanging: 'The execution of a murderer is a solemn ritual act and its object is not only to demonstrate that murder does not pay, but that it is shameful. The penalty is not only death but death with ignominy. The death penalty fulfils this role in an unequalled way because of the quasi-religious sense of awe that attaches to it.' The Bishop of Exeter believed that it was not a sense of awe, but something far more pernicious: 'The imposition of the death sentence creates in the community a certain morbid and unhealthy excitement which is bad for general morals.' Lord Chief Justice Goddard, who had sentenced Derek Bentley to death, made his own inimitable contribution:

> There was a dreadful case a few weeks ago of a little spinster, four feet nine inches in height, living on the edge of some mining village, and so afraid of being attacked that she had all the windows of her cottage screwed up. A young brute of about 23 broke into that house. He battered that poor little creature to death; all her ribs were broken, and he cut her throat. All he got out of it was a small quantity of rather trivial jewellery. Are those people to be kept alive?

As Koestler had feared, the House of Lords defeated the Bill. Ninety-five members voted in favour, with 238 against.

The following week the front-page leader in the *New Statesman and Nation* denounced the Lords: 'The House of Lords may have delayed the abolition of hanging, but it has hastened its own abolition. From the hills and forests of darkest Britain they came: the halt, the lame, the deaf, the obscure, the senile and the forgotten – the hereditary peers of England united in their determination to use their medieval powers to retain a medieval institution.'

In October 1956 the National Campaign for the Abolition of Capital Punishment presented a petition to the Prime Minister calling on the Government to legislate for the abolition of capital punishment. It was signed by 2,500 of the great and the good – lawyers, trade unionists, writers, artists, actors, newspaper editors and members of the clergy. One of the signatories was Christmas Humphreys, who had prosecuted Ruth Ellis. The Suez crisis was in full swing and the Government was under pressure, but they were determined not to give any ground to the abolitionists. In theory the Parliament Act would have allowed for the Abolition Bill to be brought before Parliament in the next session and, even if the Lords had rejected it again, the bill would have automatically become law, provided that a year had passed since it was first introduced. But the Government didn't have to invoke the Parliament Act and of course they chose not to; instead they quickly introduced legislation that would amend the law of murder but still retain hanging for some types of murder. It was a deliberate tactic to prevent the Commons from voting again on the issue of straight abolition. The Government calculated that if the Homicide Bill could be forced through the Commons quickly enough, it would kill off the Abolition Bill. The Homicide Bill was published on 7 November 1956 and it became law in March 1957. During the bill's passage through Parliament, Eden resigned, Harold Macmillan became Prime Minister and Gwilym Lloyd-George lost his job as Home Secretary.

The Homicide Act was ill conceived and the attempt to impose a logical distinction between capital and non-capital murder was a disaster. Capital murder meant murder committed in the furtherance of theft, whilst resisting or avoiding arrest; murder of a police officer or prison officer; and murder by shooting or causing an explosion. If someone stabbed a woman to death they would not be hanged, but if they stole her handbag and then stabbed her to death, they would. The first execution under the Homicide Act was carried out in July 1957, after an interlude of almost two years when there had been no hangings because the question of abolition was being debated in Parliament. It was another eight years before capital punishment was finally outlawed. During those eight years twenty-eight people were hanged.

CHAPTER THIRTEEN

The End

Pierrepoint worked as an executioner for twenty-four years and then, in 1974, eighteen years after his last execution, he published his autobiography and announced his conversion to the anti-hanging lobby. He was stripped of his mystery and finally, it seems, he lost his faith. The hangman turns against the death penalty – an ironic twist in this particularly English dance of the macabre, and a fantastic marketing opportunity. Pierrepoint's autobiography was published at a time when the IRA bombing campaign had revived a national debate on the re-introduction of capital punishment for terrorist murders; in the same year the House of Commons had defeated a motion to restore the death penalty for terrorist murders by a majority of 129. It was eighteen years since Pierrepoint had resigned from his post as the official executioner, but he was still in demand and he still had a role to play: now he was the retired executioner, affable, quotable, always interested in a fee.

Pierrepoint's new role seemed to fit in comfortably with the rest of his life; the Pierrepoints lived in 'Ivanhoe', a detached bungalow on the outskirts of Southport, and during the late 1950s and early 1960s they were still running the Rose and

Crown. Pierrepoint was a keen gardener and Tommy Mann remembers that he enjoyed presenting his friends and neighbours with flowers from his garden, especially the ladies. The Pierrepoints kept a donkey and 'Uncle Albert' took Tommy Mann's children for rides around the garden. They were entertained by Pierrepoint's magic tricks (Tommy Mann's daughter still has Pierrepoint's bendy wand) and he took them for days out in Blackpool. The Pierrepoints loved children and it was not only Tommy's children who enjoyed their hospitality; Nicola Rossi's parents ran an ice cream shop in Southport: 'Albert and Anne were among the most decent and straightforward people I have ever met.' She remembers the paddling pool in the garden and the roses that Pierrepoint would cut for her mother, 'with the thorns carefully removed'.

Pierrepoint gave up the licence at the Rose and Crown in the 1960s and took on seasonal work at the main post office in Southport, helping to sort the letters at Christmas. Tommy Mann could never really understand why Pierrepoint did this: he had done very well out of the Rose and Crown and he was good with money, interested in making money. He wasn't a great reader, although he was a bit of a hypochondriac and he had a large collection of medical books, but he pored over the financial pages and boasted to Tommy that he and Anne would be well provided for, even if they lived to be a hundred. So why the menial work at the post office? Perhaps he was still troubled by the poverty of his childhood and his memories of his father's desperate attempts to keep the family afloat, or perhaps he enjoyed the company.

Cyril Moss is a retired postman who lives in Southport. He first met Pierrepoint in the 1950s when he went into the Rose and Crown: 'He had a big cigar in his mouth. I thought, you don't look like a hangman to me. The locals told me he had hanged a man that morning in Leeds. I would never have guessed it, he was so jovial.'

Later, when Pierrepoint came to work at the post office, Cyril got to know him much better. He says that Pierrepoint had a great sense of humour: 'He was always one of the lads.' But he was also a courteous man: 'A real gentleman, always doffed his cap.' Cyril and his wife went to tea with the Pierrepoints on a couple of occasions and he remembers Anne with great fondness: 'A lovely, lovely girl. A dream of a woman. Never interfered, never bothered. I don't think she asked him about his work. She was a very shy, reserved woman.' Cyril seemed genuinely pleased to have an opportunity to speak about his old friend: 'Albert was a lovely man. You would never dream he'd done that job ... You couldn't get a nicer couple.'

Pierrepoint liked people and he enjoyed having an audience – playing with the children in the garden, showing off his magic tricks, the stints at the post office, helping Tommy Mann out behind the bar at his pub, meeting up with his old friends in the police force and the prison service, dropping in at the Conservative club in Southport for a drink and a chat – he was rarely on his own and he was always entertaining somebody. Alongside all of this he still had a public role to play and a wider audience to reach: the Homicide Act of 1957 was becoming increasingly controversial and more controversy meant more publicity for the retired executioner. In 1961 seven people were executed for capital murder and Ludovic Kennedy's book *Ten Rillington Place* was published. In the same year Pierrepoint appeared in the opening moments of a BBC documentary, *The Death Penalty*.

The programme is thinly disguised as a neutral investigation into the pros and cons of capital punishment, but in fact it delivers a devastating critique of the death penalty. The introduction is worth quoting in full:

> England prides itself on being the most gentle country in the world. [Picture of couple picnicking by river with dog, bells ringing, probably Cambridge.] We are tolerant, we forgive easily, we care for what is small and helpless. [Cut to men fishing and mothers with large prams in a playground.] We detest violence as a foreign vulgarity. [Cut to idyllic village-green cricket match.] But in fact the violence is deep within in us and strong. And we enjoy it more than we know when it comes at second hand. [Cut to football match, not idyllic, crowds shouting.] Our children grow up to think *this* is funny [cut to Punch and Judy on beach, children cheering as Punch is hanged] and they accept *this* as an afternoon treat [cut to Chamber of Horrors]. We are masters of the murder story and our crime reporting is at once the wonder and the bewilderment of the world. A picturesque murder is a national event and we retain a violent and ignoble death for our convicted murderers. [Actor's voice speaks the words of the death sentence in sombre tones.] Before we consider whether we should hang men and women, here precisely is what is done to them. These facts were given in evidence before the Royal Commission. [Cut to head and shoulders shot of Pierrepoint, speaking to the camera.] 'My name is Albert Pierrepoint and I was an executioner for twenty five years.'

Pierrepoint's tone and accent – down to earth, distinctly

northern – come as a bit of a relief after the relentless gravitas of the received pronunciation voiceover.

Pierrepoint reads an edited version of his evidence to the Royal Commission, explaining exactly what his duties were from the moment he entered the prison. He is wearing a suit and tie and a pair of reading glasses and most of the time he is looking down at his script. When he has finished the voiceover swings back into action, more portentous by the minute: 'And so, behind these walls [gloomy shot of Victorian prison gates], in awful secrecy, the servants of the public carry out the public's will. They dispose of a human being. And if the crime has made the front page of the newspapers, we follow each detail of his fate as closely as we can.'

This was 1961: wages and crime were increasing, the Beatles were about to release their first record and the white heat of the technological revolution was just around the corner. *Lady Chatterley* was no longer considered obscene, the cultural and political certainties of the post-war years were under attack and a new, progressive consensus was emerging. Interestingly, the opening sequence of *The Death Penalty* invokes the spirit of the early 1950s, the time of the Festival of Britain and the Coronation, when it was still possible to talk about a collective national identity. Humphrey Jennings' film, commissioned by the Festival Committee, began like this: 'Perhaps because we in Britain live on a group of small islands, we like to think of ourselves as a family.' The opening of *The Death Penalty* sets up the idea of a certain kind of Britishness, represented by cricket, in order to undermine it and expose the latent violence in the culture, represented by football. In 1961 football was a solidly working-class sport and the suggestion that there was a connection between strong emotions at football matches and a national proclivity for state killing now seems ridiculous; apart from anything else, the parliamentary advocates of capital punishment were much more likely to be found at Lords than Wembley. Pierrepoint belonged to the football classes; he would have resented the inference.

The programme goes on to address the question of public opinion: 'Most people are in favour, probably, of the retention of the death penalty.' An hour later, after countless interviews with people in the know, the audience is left in no doubt at all that 'most people' are wrong. The voiceover returns: 'We have on purpose given no final verdict.' The BBC was educating its audience, in true patrician style, and Pierrepoint had been very useful. He had been paraded as a gruesomely authentic exhibit in a different kind of Chamber of Horrors, explaining how he 'dispose[d] of a human being'. In some ways, this was the Royal Commission all over again – in 1950 it was politically expedient for the Government to lift the veil of secrecy that surrounded the official executioner, and they were indifferent to the effect this might have on Pierrepoint; in 1961 Pierrepoint was wheeled out to repeat what he had said in 1950, but this time he was used for a different political agenda. Of course the difference was that in 1961 Pierrepoint had a genuine choice: he could have refused the invitation.

Despite a steady increase in crime during the 1960s, and the popular, but mistaken, perception that Britain was suffering from an epidemic of violent crime (not helped by the Great Train Robbery in 1963), the total number of people executed between 1962 and 1964 was seven, in marked contrast to the preceding three years, when the total was sixteen. The death penalty was still legal, but in practice it was becoming an anachronism.

On 7 July 1964 two dairymen from Preston, Peter Allen, aged twenty-one, and Gwynne Evans, aged twenty-four, were convicted of murder in the course of a robbery and sentenced to death. The case did not get much coverage in the national press but it was front-page news in Pierrepoint's local paper, the *Lancashire Evening Post*: 'Preston Men Sentenced to Die – Wife led weeping from court as husband goes below.' A Preston branch of the National Campaign for the Abolition of Capital Punishment was set up and a petition for clemency was signed by hundreds of people. Local MPs, including Julian Amery, the brother of John Amery and MP for Preston North, were called upon to make their own views on capital punishment public, but it didn't make any difference: the Home Secretary, Henry Brooke, did not grant a reprieve. The two men were executed at eight o'clock in the morning on 13 August 1964, Allen at Walton Gaol in Liverpool and Evans at Strangeways in Manchester. In the Market Square in Preston twenty-four people stood in silence to mark the moment of the executions.

Two months later the Labour Party came to power and Harold Wilson appointed Lord Gardiner as Lord Chancellor, and Sir Frank Soskice, a committed abolitionist, as Home Secretary. Sydney Silverman introduced the Murder (Abolition of Death Penalty) Bill in December 1964; there were no prisoners awaiting execution and nobody could be sentenced to death while the bill was being debated. The debate was opened by Silverman, who spoke for over an hour without any notes, and the Commons voted in favour of abolition by a majority of 185. The issue no longer split MPs along predictable party political lines: eighty Conservatives voted in favour of abolition. (Margaret Thatcher was one of the Conservatives who voted against abolition.) In July the Lords debated the bill; this time, the Lord

Chancellor, the Lord Chief Justice and the Archbishop of Canterbury all spoke in favour of abolition. The Lords had voted against abolition in 1948 and again in 1956. On 15 July 1965 they voted in favour, by a majority of one hundred. In November of that year the bill became law and the death penalty was abolished, initially for a period of five years. In 1968 Sydney Silverman died and a year later abolition was made permanent.

The two men from Preston, Peter Allen and Gwynne Evans, were the last people to be executed in the United Kingdom. For years high treason and 'piracy with violence' were left on the statute books as capital crimes and finally, in 1990, the Criminal Justice Act swept away this anachronism: 'No person shall suffer death for any offence.'

The IRA bombing campaign of the 1970s led to regular calls for the re-introduction of the death penalty and although the majority of MPs were against re-introduction, the issue did not go away. The year 1978 was a particularly busy one for Pierrepoint. In February the motion proposed at the Cambridge Union Debating Society was: 'This House would restore the death penalty.' The guest speakers in favour of the motion were Teddy Taylor MP and Group Captain Douglas Bader. Speaking against the motion were Dick Taverne MP and Pierrepoint. The invitation had been issued by the President of the Debating Society, Andrew Mitchell, now Conservative MP for Sutton Coldfield and Shadow Minister for International Development. He remembers that the audience was riveted by Pierrepoint, who spoke with great confidence. Afterwards, he took Pierrepoint for a drink (he drank half pints of lager) and they talked until two in the morning: 'At one point I looked at him and realised that his eyes were completely dead.'

The Vice-President of the Debating Society was Robert Harris, now a successful novelist. His recollection of Pierrepoint's speech is slightly different:

> He read out his speech very carefully and there was an embarrassing moment when he reached the bottom of one page, and fumbled to turn over to the next. As luck would have it, the words on which he finished the page were 'during the course of my work I met many interesting people … ' – and then there was this long, long pause, into which of course some wit shouted out '… and hanged them!'

Robert Harris also remembers the moment when Pierrepoint shook his hand: 'He had the strongest handshake I've ever experienced; I was left looking at my whitened, compressed fingers.' The Secretary of the Debating Society was Daniel Janner, now a QC, and he had the job of collecting Pierrepoint from Cambridge station and taking him in a taxi to the Union: 'I asked him why he decided to be a hangman. He said: "So I could travel and meet people", which I found rather interesting … ' There were more than 600 people in the audience at the Cambridge Union and the record shows that Pierrepoint spoke for twenty minutes. It was the longest speech of the evening. The motion to restore the death penalty was rejected by a majority of 437.

Four months after this debate Pierrepoint appeared on a television programme about capital punishment. *Tonight* was a studio discussion chaired by Robin Day. Four politicians sat on one side of the studio and put the arguments for and against capital punishment. Robin Day then put these opinions to a panel of experts on the other side of the studio. Jim Jardine, of the Police Federation, and Peter Waugh, of the Police Officers Association, both advocated restoration of the death penalty for particular offences. Louis Blom-Cooper QC, Chairman of the Howard League for Penal Reform, and Dr Richard Clutterbuck from the University of Essex put forward the arguments against capital punishment. Robin Day turned to Pierrepoint and quoted his own book at him: 'As a retired executioner, you have written that, "I now sincerely hope that no man is called upon to carry out another execution in my country." Why?' Pierrepoint coughed, shifted in his seat and looked around the studio. He was visibly uneasy: 'Well, when I started writing that book … our country was very quiet … First, I'd like to say that I respect the Prison … ' At this point Robin Day interrupted, clearly irritated that Pierrepoint was not saying what he was expected to say. He attempted to pin him down, with no success. Eventually he became impatient and barked at him, 'Are you in favour of it?' Pierrepoint clearly felt extremely uncomfortable: 'I'm not committing myself … I had a friend, a policeman, shot in Blackpool, you see … ' Robin Day lost interest and Reginald Maudling MP, a former Conservative Home Secretary, stepped in gleefully to score a political point.

This programme reveals the enduring complexity of Pierrepoint's public role. As the official executioner, his part had been rewritten without his permission. In his retirement he seized the opportunity to write his own script, to subvert the narrative. As a result, he was invited into the heart of the Establishment, the place where all the Newsams and the Maxwell Fyfes had come from. He was a catch, a curiosity, the bearded lady in the debating chamber. Then he was asked to appear on television and say the same thing again. He had yet another public role: the hangman who had turned. But this time it wasn't so simple. This time he was sitting next to two men who represented the police and the prison officers, who represented Daws and all the staff at Strangeways. These people admired and respected Pierrepoint the executioner, not Pierrepoint the speaker at the Cambridge Union. Where did his loyalties lie? For or against? Pierrepoint was unable, literally, to answer the question.

At the end of the year Pierrepoint was in demand again. This time it was Madame Tussauds in London who wanted his help. They were refurbishing the Chamber of Horrors and they asked Pierrepoint if he would come down to London to advise them on the correct way to assemble the gallows. Pierrepoint was happy to help in theory, but negotiating the right terms proved difficult. Madame Tussauds offered to pay a consultancy fee and travelling expenses. Pierrepoint was outraged: he considered the fee too low and he couldn't understand how they expected him to do a 500-mile round trip without an overnight stay: 'I was completely disgusted … I have been in London many times this year, on television programmes and interviews [and] without any trouble I demand £200 plus all expenses.' Eventually they managed to settle on a figure that satisfied Pierrepoint and he gave them the benefit of his expertise. (In 1996 Pierrepoint himself appeared in the Chamber of Horrors for the first time. Today he is still on display, caught in the act of executing John Christie.)

A year later Pierrepoint was back in the news. On 16 July 1979, twenty-four years and a few days after the execution of her sister, Muriel Jakubait met Albert Pierrepoint in a hotel in Knightsbridge and together they visited Ellis's grave. It was like a grotesque game of consequences, played by sadistic children with an unhealthy interest in new forms of human suffering:

'Ruth Ellis's sister met Ruth Ellis's executioner in/at/on/under … She said to him …' In a way it *was* a game of consequences, played by a national newspaper with an unhealthy interest in its own circulation figures. The meeting was engineered by the *Sun*, and the hook was an impending parliamentary vote on the re-introduction of hanging. Terrorist murders in Northern Ireland were an increasing concern and factions within the Conservative Party were advocating the reinstatement of the death penalty. Margaret Thatcher and her cabinet were in favour of re-introduction, with the notable exception of the Home Secretary, William Whitelaw. (The possibility of re-introduction was taken very seriously: in May of the same year the Governor of Wandsworth prison asked the Works Department to tell him what they would need to do in order to reinstate the execution chamber and the condemned cell.)

The paper carried a double page spread with a large photograph of Pierrepoint standing by Ellis's grave, wearing a dark suit, hands clasped behind his back, head bowed. The caption under the photograph reads: 'Ex-hangman Albert Pierrepoint at the grave of Ruth Ellis – the last woman to be executed in Britain. Pierrepoint did the job. MPs could restore capital punishment on Thursday. But Pierrepoint is praying that they won't.' The *Sun's* story was that Pierrepoint, now passionately anti-hanging, had long wanted to visit Ellis's grave and was waiting for permission from her sister Muriel: 'She gave it at a meeting in a Knightsbridge hotel – but she refused to shake his hand.' Pierrepoint was quoted advancing all the standard arguments against the re-introduction of capital punishment: it represents the desire for revenge, not justice; it does not work as a deterrent; it will not discourage terrorists and in fact it will make them into martyrs: 'Let's bury the rope for ever.'

The *Sun* liked the fact that Pierrepoint had earned his views, unlike the lily-livered politicians debating in Parliament. Usefully for the newspaper, he was still angry with the Establishment: 'There are politicians baying for the return of the death penalty. But would they do the job themselves? Would they pull the lever releasing the trap door? Would they permit their sons or daughters to do it? Would they want to see for themselves the convicted murderer's journey into the unknown? *Or do they still prefer to leave the dirty work to someone else*?'

On 19 July 1979 the House of Commons rejected the reinstatement of the death penalty by a majority of 119. In her book, published in 2005, Muriel Jakubait said that she was hijacked by the *Sun* and that she had never agreed to meet Pierrepoint. In a radio interview in 1987 Pierrepoint spoke about the meeting. He was slightly incoherent and his version is at odds with Muriel Jakubait's version. This was how he described the visit to the grave:

> We went to see where she was buried, you see, and she was at the end of a row, with the wall beside her, and I was just looking at it and I took my hat off and all that, and all of a sudden we heard some bugger groaning – aaahhh – and we thought she was coming up from the grave, you know [he laughs] and it was a fella, drunk as a bloody clot, hidden behind the back and we didn't see him until we went round the back.

Whatever the truth behind this bizarre meeting, the story in the *Sun* undoubtedly revived interest in Pierrepoint's new public role as the hangman who was against capital punishment. In real life he was a retired publican who worked in the post office in Southport every Christmas, helping to sort the letters. He was invited to the annual carol concert at Strangeways prison and he was popular with local police officers, but he didn't belong to the association for retired executioners, because there wasn't one.

Pierrepoint had hanged more than 400 people on behalf of the state but when the state no longer condoned hanging, the hangman ceased to exist. It was all very democratic, very restrained, very English. He wasn't branded a mass murderer and he wasn't silenced by secrecy legislation, he was simply ignored. The state had grown up and it didn't want to be reminded of its youthful misdemeanours. Since the Government was not prepared to give him a pension, what else could be done? The media stepped in to fill the gap.

Tommy Mann says that in the 1980s Pierrepoint began to suffer from symptoms of dementia. He was sporadically forgetful and irrational and gradually this jovial, sociable man became more isolated. Old friends in the police had always been regular visitors at 'Ivanhoe', but when he became ill Pierrepoint developed the habit of ringing the police station after his visitors had left, alleging that they had stolen money from his safe. It was all very awkward and eventually the visits stopped. Slowly the dementia took hold and although Anne tried to protect him, Pierrepoint became increasingly irrational and vulnerable.

Tommy describes Pierrepoint's decline with great sadness and blames the disease for Pierrepoint's preoccupation with money; he had always been very interested in money, but in Tommy's opinion the dementia transformed his interest into an overwhelming anxiety. Tommy believes that it was this anxiety that drove Pierrepoint to take the suitcase out from underneath the bed and sell off his hangman's memorabilia. He says that Anne felt that it was wrong to sell, and she was particularly upset about the execution diaries, but Pierrepoint knew that people would pay for his artefacts and he was determined to make a profit. After all those years of silence, Anne couldn't prevent him from getting on the train to London – it was what he had always done.

Anne became ill herself and while she was in hospital Pierrepoint was unable to manage on his own. He was admitted to a different hospital and the separation made them both miserable; when Anne was well enough they were reunited in the Melvin Nursing Home in Southport, where they shared a large room on the ground floor. Mostly, he was left alone, but in 1991 the *News of the World* printed a large photograph of Pierrepoint, looking frail and gaunt in a large overcoat that hung about his shrunken frame, flanked by two nurses, apparently out for a walk. The caption told the story: 'Twilight Years of a Haunted Hangman … The ghost of the gallows has come to haunt Britain's most famous hangman.' According to the newspaper, Pierrepoint was 'stricken with remorse', but Tommy Mann saw him regularly when he was in the nursing home and he doesn't remember any remorse, only the increasing incoherence of his dementia.

I went to see the house, which is no longer a nursing home. It is large, detached and double-fronted, with bay windows and white pebble-dash, in an expensive part of town, popular with footballers and their wives. The window to the left of the front door was the Pierrepoints' room. Tommy says that they were happy when they were together, even though they had left behind 'Ivanhoe', with its donkey and its lovely garden.

Pierrepoint died on 10 July 1992 at the Melvin Nursing Home. He was eighty-seven. His death certificate records that the cause of death was bronchopneumonia and Alzheimer's disease. His occupation was given as 'Publican (retired)'. Patricia Wynne, matron and owner of the nursing home, told the *Lancashire Evening Post* that Pierrepoint had died peacefully: 'He was a perfect gentleman who loved singing, old time waltzing and going for walks.' The *News of the World* announced that the 'King of the rope dies' and Pierrepoint's death was front-page news in the *Southport Visitor*: 'Executioner! Peaceful end for the man of death.' The funeral was held at Southport crematorium and the hearse was accompanied by police outriders. The media were out in force and the police, loyal to the end, closed the gates of the crematorium to prevent the television crews and photographers getting in. Tommy Mann gave the eulogy and the hymn was 'The Rugged Cross'. Tommy sang 'A Little Bitty Tear', originally by Burl Ives. It was his friend's favourite song. Pierrepoint's ashes were scattered in the Memorial Gardens.

After Pierrepoint's death, Anne was worried that she wouldn't have enough money to pay for her own nursing care. She sold 'Ivanhoe', along with all their furniture and most of their possessions, but she kept a photograph of Pierrepoint in her room. She died five years later, at the age of ninety-three.

*

In May 1992, two months before Pierrepoint died, Christie's auction house in South Kensington sold what was described as the 'Albert Pierrepoint Collection' from the Forman Archive of Crime and Punishment. The collection included leg irons, manacles, ropes and plaster life masks of Pierrepoint and one of his assistants, Syd Dernley. Pierrepoint's execution diaries were sold for £19,800. Aficionados of crime and punishment memorabilia speak of Pierrepoint's execution diaries as if they are the crown jewels. Perhaps it is the term that is so alluring: 'execution diaries', holding out the promise of a description of the indescribable. In fact they are not diaries in a personal sense, but a record of each execution that Pierrepoint performed. Pierrepoint had followed the example set by his father, who had kept his own execution diary, as well as filling two thick notebooks with his handwritten memoirs. When Henry died he left Pierrepoint all his papers and Pierrepoint read the execution diary when he was seventeen. Henry's diary was not confined to the details of his executions – he included a record of the birth of all his children – but Pierrepoint decided that his own diary would be a strictly professional record.

According to *The Times*, 'The buyer [of the diaries] was a diminutive racing tipster who … enjoyed lighting a cigar in imitation of his hero, Mr Pierrepoint.' Pierrepoint's life mask was bought by a Mr Elton M. Hyder Junior by telephone for £3,410. (Hyder was an American lawyer who acted as a special prosecutor in the trials of Japanese war criminals in Tokyo after the war and built up a vast collection which is now displayed in the University of Texas School of Law. According to its website, 'The Hyder collection illustrates the history, tradition, and majesty of the law.')

Two men were watching the sale with particular interest: Syd Dernley, Pierrepoint's former assistant, and Fernand Meysonnier, who was the official executioner in Algeria between 1948 and 1962. Meysonnier used the guillotine and he claims to have executed 200 Algerians. He was at Christies to buy artefacts for his museum in the south of France. The report in the *The Times* goes on: 'M. Meysonnier said he would not be displaying anything tasteless. The human head of one of his victims, preserved in formaldehyde, will be kept at home.' After the sale Syd Dernley and Monsieur Meysonnier were introduced to each other and they retired to a hotel lounge to swap memories. The report in *The Times* was tantalising; what was the Forman Archive?

The website was easy to find: 'Presenting 20th Century History from Forman Archive … Enquiries from Film and Television Companies welcome.' There was a range of videos and CDs *Germany Calling, Nazi Radio Propaganda*, reduced from £13.95 to £8, and *Dr Goebbels Jazz Orchestra, Propaganda Swing*, now 'SOLD OUT'), including something called *Hangman's Tales, The Pierrepoints*, reduced from £13.95 to £9.99. The hangman video came with a warning: 'You will see two executions and human remains which some may find shocking and disturbing.' It also promised a video interview with Pierrepoint. I wanted to see this interview, but I was worried about buying the video. Was this legitimate research, or would I be crossing an invisible line, compromising myself, becoming a sadistic voyeur? I decided to wait and mull it over. Three months later I was convinced that buying the video was a perfectly reasonable thing to do. I was battle-weary by now and I had grown another skin. Hanging was my daily fare. I told myself that my earlier scruples were ill-conceived; clearly I had to see the video in order to compare this recording of Pierrepoint with the many others I had now seen. This wasn't voyeurism, it was biography.

I watched the video: the interview with Pierrepoint covered ground that was familiar to me and it was accompanied by interviews with Syd Dernley, assistant executioner, and 'the last Assistant Executioner still alive today'. The rest was a curious miscellany of gruesome facts and images: Chinese executions by the sword during the Boxer rebellion in 1901, the Nuremberg executions and an interview with Monsieur Meysonnier, the French executioner. I found some of the material horrifying and repulsive and I wished that I hadn't watched it. But I still didn't know how Pierrepoint and the Formans had met, how this video had come about. Where did the Formans fit in? I wrote to them, asking whether I could talk to them about their relationship with Pierrepoint and the history of their archive. In reply they explained that they were very busy: their archives generated a huge workload and they had to answer endless queries. For these reasons they had decided to charge for interviews. If I would like to meet them, it would cost £200. I hesitated, but not for long. After all, I had crossed the Rubicon when I bought the video.

Bromsgrove is a large town in the West Midlands. It is twinned with Gronau in Germany and is the home of Michael and Doreen Forman. The Formans are in their seventies and they met Pierrepoint when he was in his seventies. Michael Forman is a collector. He started out selling old coins and moved on to medals. Now his collection includes the orders and medals of Kaiser Wilhelm II, the papers of Nazi propagandist E. R. Dietze, archives from Colditz and Nuremberg, and what he describes as an 'excessively rare Hess archive'. He has photographs, royal relics, coronets and, he tells me, a man trap. Forman says that in the 1970s he bought the archive of William Joyce, 'Lord Haw Haw'. He was keen to add to this new collection so he wrote to the man who had executed Joyce, wondering whether he had anything of interest. Pierrepoint couldn't help with Joyce, but he did offer Forman something else: his own 'collection'. Michael Forman says that Pierrepoint's collection consisted of 'hundreds of documents', the equipment he used for executions, and his execution diaries.

Pierrepoint visited them regularly at their antiques shop in Piccadilly and they went up to stay with Pierrepoint and Anne in Southport. They were not just business associates, they were friends. Anne never accompanied Pierrepoint on his visits to London but when they stayed at 'Ivanhoe' she chatted with Doreen while the men talked business. He didn't want her to know what was happening. Anne would never talk about his job, she didn't want anything to do with 'the nasty side' of things, but she enjoyed his celebrity status, and she liked the money. Anne was working as a nurse when she met Pierrepoint but she didn't work after they were married, he wouldn't have wanted her to, although Anne was the one who kept the accounts.

Doreen describes Pierrepoint as a flirt; she says he was always singing to the ladies, presenting them with bunches of roses from the garden. He was small and dapper, never a hair out of place. Grimacing, Doreen tells me that Pierrepoint confided in her that women were attracted to him because of his job. Anne turned a blind eye and Doreen thinks that underneath it all Pierrepoint was devoted to his wife. I ask about the dementia. They remember this in a different way to Tommy Mann. He thinks that it crept up slowly, over ten years or so. The Formans think that it started much later, just a few years before he died. They have never met Tommy Mann.

Over the years the collection grew. The Formans filmed their conversations with Pierrepoint and they took him to an art school in Birmingham for a mould to be made of his face and hands. These were cast in plaster and later in bronze. A life mask. I ask Michael Forman why he had these things made: 'Because he was the greatest executioner in the world.' Then he shows me Pierrepoint's right hand, cast in bronze. A small hand with neatly cut nails, cupped in an upright position, the fingers curving inward slightly. My own hand is much bigger and I reach out to grasp Pierrepoint's hand. I wonder if this might be a significant moment, but as I hold his hand in mine all I can feel is the deep, ancient chill of the bronze. The clouds don't part in Bromsgrove, there is no revelation. Doreen brings in cheese sandwiches and a bowl of crisps.

*

In November 2005, at about the same time that I watched the Formans' video, a man called Fred Wright appeared on the *Antiques Roadshow* with a collection of documents relating to Pierrepoint, including a book that was described as Pierrepoint's execution diary. Fred Wright said that Pierrepoint had been a close friend and that he had given him all these papers and documents. The expert described it as a 'fascinating and very important' collection with a 'very, very limited market'. He estimated that the collection might fetch between £3,000 and £5,000 at auction, possibly much more if you got the right people on the right day. He hoped that it would be preserved for posterity, since it was an important part of our history.

My meeting with Fred Wright took a long time to set up. I made phone calls to people who said they could put me in touch, but somehow they were all hesitant, as if there might be a problem. No one said there *was* a problem but I didn't feel happy about it. Mostly I was annoyed with myself: this man had just appeared on prime-time television, displaying his wares, and yet I couldn't track him down. Just as I was beginning to despair I got a phone call from a very senior retired police officer who told me that he had known Fred Wright for more than twenty years. He said that he would set up a meeting for me. Not only that, he would escort me to the meeting and make the introduction himself.

I arrived at Manchester Piccadilly on a cold November morning. My escort was waiting for me at the end of the platform. He was a tall, thin man with an intelligent, ruddy face. He was wearing a dark overcoat and his shoes were perfectly polished. He drove me through the centre of Manchester and out into the suburbs. He was interested in Pierrepoint, like all police and prison officers of a certain age. He thought that he had met him once, but it wasn't a big deal at the time. He said that as a practising Christian he was opposed to capital punishment, but he thought that if the police force were asked if they wanted the return of the death penalty, the answer would be yes. He was softly spoken, with a lilting accent and I felt that he thought very carefully before he spoke. As we got nearer to Fred Wright's house he had to consult the map, which meant pulling over. It would have been easier if I had read the map while he drove, but I didn't suggest it.

In the rain we turned into Fred Wright's street: detached houses and generous driveways, part of a development that must once have boasted of 'executive homes'. There were no real front gardens and very few trees, just plenty of space around the brick and the concrete. The miserly November light made every thing look flat and washed out; there no longer seemed to be three dimensions. The car slowed down and we started looking for Fred Wright's house. Suddenly we saw something surprising: a cluster of tall, dark trees, probably fir trees. Behind them was a house. Fred Wright's house. We parked by the kerb, leaving the driveway and the car-port free.

Fred Wright had grey hair and an unhealthy looking complexion.

I noticed that he wasn't wearing any shoes and he had slim feet. We stood on the threshold of his house in the semi-darkness and I introduced myself. His hands looked swollen, clumps of tight flesh. Before we sat down he took us into the back room. It was a large, cold room and the walls were lined with dark-brown cork tiles. In the middle of the room was a full-size snooker table, covered with a cloth. The cloth was pink, with tints of beige. A vase full of pale pink plastic roses, more dusty than blousy, had been placed in the centre of the table, too far away to reach. In one corner of the room there was a cocktail bar, well stocked with liqueurs. In another corner was a dresser full of trophies, trinkets, photographs and a collection of costume dolls. Along one wall was a long wooden bench. On the bench there were two enormous cuddly toys – Winnie the Pooh and Tigger – both about two foot high. As we left I noticed a camera fixed onto the ceiling. I couldn't be sure, but it looked like a CCTV camera.

Fred Wright invited me to sit down on the sofa and he sat across from me in a large armchair. The sofa was covered with something shiny that looked a bit like leather and I found myself sliding around, unable to keep my notebook steady on my knees. I didn't feel very stable. The retired police officer sat on the other side of the room in another armchair. He was facing Fred Wright, but I couldn't catch his eye without turning my head towards him and away from Fred Wright, so I had no idea what he made of it all. The lights were not on and I had the impression that it was getting darker in the room as time passed, although it was only the middle of the morning. Once, Fred Wright got up and switched on the lights. Later he switched them off, for no apparent reason. Once, he changed his position, throwing his legs over the arms of the chair. Occasionally he leapt to his feet, animated by a story that he was telling, acting it out, doing the voices. He is a great talker.

In 1967, when Fred Wright was a young prison officer in Strangeways, Pierrepoint came to the prison. He had been retired for more than ten years and this was a social visit to see Norman Brown, the Deputy Governor. He was a regular at the carol concerts in Strangeways and the prison officers had a lot of respect for the Pierrepoint family. Fred Wright was asked to park Pierrepoint's car and they started chatting. According to Wright, this was the start of a friendship that was to last for the rest of Pierrepoint's life, a friendship that became a kind of father–son relationship, a great source of happiness for Wright, who was brought up in children's homes, and for Pierrepoint, who had no children of his own. Pierrepoint called him 'son' and Wright returned the compliment, calling him 'Dad'. Pierrepoint was kind and funny. He liked to sing. He confided in Wright, trusted him, and they discussed everything. Wright says that Pierrepoint gave him photographs and papers for his 'collection'. I asked Fred Wright about Anne, but he didn't have much to say about her; she was placid, she didn't get involved. I got the impression that he wasn't interested in Anne.

Gradually I understood what it is that Wright is really interested in: his collection, and the fact that everyone else had got Pierrepoint wrong. Wright wanted me to understand that he is the only person who knows. His collection, he believes, is priceless. The execution diaries are in the bank because they are much too valuable to keep at home. At home he has files full of letters and photographs. During our interview he handed me various letters and documents and then he leapt up and took them back before I had a chance to read them properly. I decided that I should make my position clear: I had not come to bid for information and I was not going to pay for these pieces of paper. I half expected him to end the interview immediately, but he was happy to carry on. He wouldn't let me into the inner sanctuary, but he did want to talk.

I asked him about Pierrepoint's relationship with the Home Office and he said that Pierrepoint always felt that they wanted him out of sight and out of mind. They used him whenever they needed him, and the rest of the time they didn't care. He didn't have any support, he just did the job and came home. Fred Wright identified with this, after a long career in the prison service. He told me about the idiotic behaviour of the prison authorities and the Home Office and I understood that he sees himself as a defender of the common man, standing up for the rights of the ordinary prisoner, fighting the good fight against the politicians and mandarins who haven't got a clue what prisons are really about. He despises the men in suits. He retired some years ago but he has an abiding interest in prisons. He told me that he travels widely and visits prisons wherever he goes. His last trip was to North Korea.

Wright sees himself as Pierrepoint's guardian angel, the keeper of the flame. In his mind he has created a fortress around his version of the executioner, a fortress surrounded by armies of fools, all clamouring to breach his defences. Inside his fortress there are piles of papers: letters slipped into plastic folders, photographs in albums – just like a family album, except that in this album the homely snapshots have handwritten dedications on the back, authenticating the picture. Wright wants to defend the fortress, but he also wants to throw down the drawbridge and feast with the enemy, when the moment is right. His experience on the *Antiques Roadshow* hasn't put him off and he has great plans. He believes that he could sell his collection to a university archive in America, or simply wait for the highest commercial bidder. I wonder if he might be happier if he remains inside the fortress, nursing his scorn.

The two execution diaries remain a mystery. There seems to be no doubt that Pierrepoint did make copies of the diaries before he sold them, but it is not clear to me how many copies he made, or exactly when he made them. A third diary now belongs to the Crime, Punishment and Law Archive attached to the Galleries of Justice in Nottingham. This diary is clearly a copy; inside the front cover whoever made the copy has made certain that there is no confusion: 'copy'. It was given to the museum on the understanding that the name of the donor would not be disclosed and the contents would not be copied or reproduced. The Formans explained to me that the original diary was, in itself, a kind of copy. Pierrepoint had a small pocket book which he took with him to each execution. In this pocket book he made brief notes and when he returned home he copied his notes into his execution diary, adding more detail – rather as a policeman might make a contemporaneous note of an arrest and, on his return to the station, write out a full statement. Perhaps it was the pocket book that appeared on the *Antiques Roadshow*. The mystery is another part of the story: Pierrepoint's value is still controversial.

*

Back in Bromsgrove, talking to the Formans, Michael Forman suddenly asked me if I would be interested in seeing Pierrepoint's equipment. After a long absence he reappeared with a case. It was not *the* suitcase; this was a black attaché case, more like an executive briefcase than an executioner's kit bag.

Michael Forman opened the case and, one by one, he placed each object on the table in front of me. A length of rope with a loop at the end of it, a leg strap, a white hood, folded up like a handkerchief, and a strap with a tear in one of the eyelets. I noticed that the hood was not really white; the white had faded and turned to yellow and there were black marks along the folded edges.

Without warning I had become a part of the story of the suitcase and I realised that I was not well prepared. I told Michael Forman that I found these objects disturbing. 'Well, you're a girl.' He pushed the rope towards me and invited me to touch it. It was greasy and I pulled my hand away quickly. I felt queasy and I had to force myself to concentrate on making a note of what I had seen.

Michael Forman drove me to the station. I had just missed my train and I had to wait an hour for the next one. Bromsgrove station is very quiet – two platforms and a connecting bridge. Nothing else. The trains are a welcome distraction in this desolate spot. It was a very long hour. I rang home and spoke to my children. They told me about their day: football club, double science, singing assembly. Their voices seemed to come from another world, from a place where the air was clearer. They wanted to know about my day – when would I be home? I realised that I was not going to tell them about what I had seen in Bromsgrove. When the train pulled out of the station I was overwhelmed with a sense of horror and shame. I had come closer to Pierrepoint than I had expected. I had got my hands dirty, after a fashion. It was time to shut the suitcase.

Albert Pierrepoint: 1905-1992

NOTE ON SOURCES

Much of the material relating to the trial of the German spies, John Amery, Ruth Ellis and Pierrepoint's resignation is from Home Office and Prison Commission files in the National Archive in London and these files are cited in the following pages. The description of an execution draws on Prison Commission memorandums and the Report of the Royal Commission on Capital Punishment, published in 1953.

I am particularly indebted to Brian Block and John Hostettler for their wonderfully clear account of the abolition of capital punishment, *Hanging in the Balance: A History of the Abolition of Capital Punishment in Britain*, to Steve Fielding for his meticulously researched record of Pierrepoint's executions, *Pierrepoint: A Family of Executioners: The Story of Britain's infamous Hangmen* and to Anette Ballinger for her incisive analysis of the Ruth Ellis trial in *Dead Woman Walking, Executed Women in England and Wales 1900–1955.*

Every effort has been made to trace copyright holders. The publishers would be interested to hear from any copyright holders not acknowledged.

BIBLIOGRAPHY

Books and Articles

Amery, Leo, *John Amery: An Explanation*, London, Corinthian Press, 1946.

Bailey, Brian, *Hangmen of England,* London, W. H. Allen, 1989.

Ballinger, Anette, *Dead Woman Walking, Executed Women in England and Wales 1900–1955*, Dartmouth, Ashgate, 2000.

Barnes, John and Nicholson, David, eds., *The Leo Amery Diaries, Volume 1: 1896–1929*, London, Hutchinson, 1980.

Barnes, John and Nicholson, David, eds., *The Leo Amery Diaries, Volume 2: The Empire At Bay, 1929–1945*, London, Hutchinson, 1988.

Belton, Neil, *The Good Listener, Helen Bamber: A Life Against Cruelty*, London, Weidenfeld and Nicolson, a division of The Orion Publishing Group, 1998.

Bentley, William George, *My Son's Execution*, London, W. H. Allen, 1957.

Binding, Tim, *A Perfect Execution*, London, Picador, 1996.

Bland, James, *The Common Hangman, English and Scottish Hangmen Before the Abolition of Public Executioners*, Sparkford, Zeon Books, 2001.

Block, Brian P. and Hostettler, John, *Hanging in the Balance: A*

History of the Abolition of Capital Punishment in Britain, Winchester, Waterside Press, 1997.

Body, Alfred H., *Old Road, A Lancashire Childhood, 1912–1926*, Manchester, E.J. Morten, 1974.

Brookes, Barbara, *Abortion in England, 1900–1967*, London, New York, Sydney, Croom Helm, 1988.

Butler, R. A., *The Art of the Possible: The Memoirs of Lord Butler*, London, Penguin, 1973.

Calvocoressi, Peter, *Nuremberg: The Facts, the Law and the Consequences*, London, Chatto and Windus, 1947.

Carlen, Pat, ed., *Criminal Women, Autobiographical Accounts*, Oxford, Polity Press, 1985.

Cesarani, David, *How Britain Became a Refuge for Nazi War Criminals*, London, Phoenix Press, 2001.

Cesarani, David, ed., *Holocaust: Critical Concepts in Holocaust Studies, Volume VI, The End of the 'Final Solution' and its Aftermaths*, London and New York, Routledge, 2004.

Cesarani, David, *Arthur Koestler, The Homeless Mind*, London, Heinemann, 1998.

Chuter-Ede, James ; ed. Kevin Jefferys, *Labour and the Wartime Coalition: From the Diaries of James Chuter Ede, 1941–1945*, London, The Historians' Press, 1987.

Clarke, Peter, *Hope and Glory, Britain 1900–1990*, London, Penguin, 1997.

Davies, Norman, *Europe: A History*, London, Pimlico, 1997.

Dernley, Syd with Newman, David, *The Hangman's Tale*, London, Macmillan, 1990.

Dors, Diana, *Diana Dors' A-Z of Men*, London and Sydney, Futura, 1984.

Douglas, Lawrence, *The Memory of Judgement: Making Law and History in the Trials of the Holocaust*, London and New

Haven, Yale University Press, 2001.
Douglas, Sholto with Wright, Robert, *Years of Command, The Second Volume of the Autobiography of Sholto Douglas, Marshal of the Royal Air Force, Lord Douglas of Kirtleside, GCB, MC, DFC*, London, Collins, 1966.
Eddlestone, John J., *Blind Justice: Miscarriages of Justice in Twentieth Century Britain*? Oxford and Santa Barbara, ABC-CLIO, 2000.
Ellis, John, *Diary of a Hangman*, London, Forum Press, 1997.
Ellis, Georgie with Taylor, Rod, *Ruth Ellis, My Mother*, London, Smith Gryphon, 1995.
Faber, David, *Speaking for England: Leo, Julian and John Amery – the tragedy of a political family*, London, Simon and Schuster, 2005.
Fielding, Steve, *Pierrepoint: A Family of Executioners: The Story of Britain's Infamous Hangmen*, London, John Blake, 2006.
Foucault, Michel, *Discipline and Punish: The Birth of the Prison*, trans. Alan Sheridan, Stroud, Sutton, 2004.
Hamilton, Iain, *Koestler: A Biography*, London, Secker and Warburg, 1982.
Hancock, Robert, *Ruth Ellis, The Last Woman to be Hanged*, London, Orion Books, 2000.
Henry, Joan, *Yield to the Night*, London, Victor Gollancz, 1954.
Hewison, Robert, *Culture and Consensus: England, Art and Politics since 1940*, London, Methuen, 1997.
Hoare, Oliver, ed., *Camp 020, MI5 and the Nazi Spies: The Official History of MI5's Wartime Interrogation Centre*, London, Public Record Office, 2000.
Hodgkinson, Peter and Rutherford, Andrew, eds., *Capital Punishment: Global Issues and Prospects*, Winchester, Waterside Press, 1996.

Hoggart, Richard, *The Uses of Literacy*, London, Chatto and Windus, 1957.

Hood, Roger, *The Death Penalty, A Worldwide Perspective*, Oxford, Oxford University Press, 2002.

Howard, Anthony, *RAB – The Life of R. A. Butler*, London, Jonathan Cape, 1987.

Humphreys, Christmas, *Both Sides of the Circle: The Autobiography of Christmas Humphreys*, London, George Allen and Unwin, 1978.

Jakubait, Muriel, with Weller, Monica, *Ruth Ellis: My Sister's Secret Life*, London, Constable and Robinson, 2005.

Joyce, Patrick, ed., *Class*, Oxford, Oxford University Press, 1995.

Kennedy, Ludovic, *Ten Rillington Place*, London, Victor Gollancz, 1961.

Koestler, Arthur, *Scum of the Earth*, New York, Macmillan, 1941.

Koestler, Arthur, *Arrow in the Blue, The First Volume of an Autobiography: 1903–1931*, London, Collins with Hamish Hamilton, 1952.

Koestler, Arthur, *The Invisible Writing, The Second Volume of an Autobiography: 19321–940*, London, Collins with Hamish Hamilton, 1954.

Koestler, Arthur, *Reflections on Hanging*, London, Victor Gollancz, 1956.

Koestler, Arthur and Koestler, Cynthia; ed. Harold Harris, *Stranger on the Square*, London, Abacus, 1985.

Short extracts from the above five books have been reprinted by permission of PFD on behalf of the Estate of Arthur Koestler, © as printed in the original volumes.

Levene, Mark, *Arthur Koestler*, London, Oswald Wolff, 1985.

Marks, Laurence and Van den Bergh, Tony, *Ruth Ellis: A Case of Diminished Responsibility?*, London, Penguin, 1990.
Marwick, Arthur, *Culture in Britain since 1945*, Oxford, Blackwell, 1991.
Marwick, Arthur, *British Society since 1945*, London, Penguin, 2003.
Maxwell-Fyfe, David, *Political Adventure: The Memoirs of the Earl of Kilmuir*, London, Weidenfeld and Nicolson, an imprint of The Orion Publishing Group, 1962.
McKenzie, Robert and Silver, Allan, *Angels in Marble, Working-Class Conservatives in Urban England*, London, Heinemann, 1968.
Mikes, George, *The Story of a Friendship*, London, Andre Deutsch, 1983.
Paget, Reginald and Silverman, Sydney, *Hanged – And Innocent?*, London, Victor Gollancz, 1953.
All our attempts at tracing the copyright holders of *Hanged – And Innocent?* by Reginald Paget and Sydney Silverman were unsuccessful.
Parris, John, *Most of My Murders*, London, Frederick Muller, 1960.
Perl, Gisella, *I was a Doctor in Auschwitz*, Salem, N.H., Ayer, 1992.
Phillips, Raymond, ed., *The Trial of Josef Kramer and forty-four others (The Belsen Trial)*, London, William Hodge, 1949.
Pierrepoint, Albert, *Executioner Pierrepoint: An Autobiography*, Eric Dobby Publishing, 2005.
Extracts from *Executioner Pierrepoint: An Autobiography* are reproduced with the permission of Eric Dobby Publishing.
Playfair, Giles and Sington, Derrick, *The Offenders: Society and the Atrocious Crime*, London, Secker and Warburg; reprinted

by permission of The Random House Group Ltd,1957.
Rawlinson, Peter, *A Price Too High*, London, Weidenfeld and Nicolson, 1989.
Reilly, Joanne, Belsen: *The Liberation of a Concentration Camp*, London and New York, Routledge, 1998.
Rogers, Ann, *Secrecy and Power in the British State, A History of the Official Secrets Act*, London, Pluto Press, 1997.
Sheldon, Sally, *Beyond Control: Medical Power and Abortion Law*, London and Chicago, Pluto Press, 1997.
Smart, Carol, *Ties that Bind: Law, Marriage and the Reproduction of Patriarchal Relations*, London, Routledge and Kegan Paul, 1984.
Stedman Jones, Gareth, *Languages of Class, Studies in Working Class History, 1832–1982*, Cambridge, Cambridge University Press, 1983.
Taylor, Telford, *The Anatomy of the Nuremberg Trials, A Personal Memoir*, London and New York, Bloomsbury, 1993.
Trow, M. J., *'Let Him Have It, Chris', The Murder of Derek Bentley*, London, Constable, 1990.
Tusa, Ann and Tusa, John, *The Nuremberg Trial,* London, Macmillan, 1983.
Tweg, Sue, *Not the Full Story: Representing Ruth Ellis, in Biography,* Volume 23, Number 1, Hawaii, University of Hawaii Press, 2000.
Vincent, David, *The Culture of Secrecy, Britain 1832–1998*, Oxford, Oxford University Press, 1998.
Weale, Adrian, *Patriot Traitors: Roger Casement, John Amery and the Real Meaning of Treason*, London, Viking, 2001.
West, Rebecca, *The Meaning of Treason*, London, Macmillan, 1949.
West, Rebecca, *A Train of Powder*, London, Macmillan, 1955.

Extracts from *The Meaning of Treason* (copyright © Estate of Rebecca West 1947) and *A Train of Powder* (copyright © Estate of Rebecca West 1955) by Rebecca West are reproduced by permission of PFD (www.pfd.co.uk) on behalf of the Estate of Rebecca West.
Whiting, Charles, *Hitler's Secret War*, Barnsley, Lee Cooper Pen and Sword Books, 2000.
Willis, Ted, *Dixon of Dock Green: My Life by George Dixon*, London, William Kimber, 1960.
Wise, Damon, *Come by Sunday: The fabulous, ruined life of Diana Dors*, London, Pan, 1999.

Official and Press Reports

Hansard (House of Commons Debates).
Report of the Royal Commission on Capital Punishment, 1949–1953 (HMSO, Cmnd 8932, 1953).
Minutes of Evidence of the Royal Commission on Capital Punishment, 1949–1953.
The Brabin Report, London, HMSO, 1966.
The British Imperial Calendar and Civil Service List, London, HMSO, 1956.
R v Ellis (Ruth) [2003] EWCA Crim. 3556.
R v Bentley (Deceased) [2001] 1 Cr. App. R. 307.

National Archives, London

Chapter One: PCOM 8/196, PCOM 9/626, HO 144/22510; Chapter Three: KV 2/1452, KV 2/1700, KV 2/1699; Chapter Four: PCOM 9/633; Chapter Five: HO 144/22823; Chapter Nine: HO 291/237; Chapter Ten: MEPO 2/9888; Chapter

Eleven: HO 291/238, FO 371/116897; Chapter Twelve: PCOM 9/1773, PCOM 9/2024.

National Sound Archive, London

Interview with Albert Pierrepoint, broadcast by Red Rose Radio (Preston) 1987.

Mass Observation Archive, Sussex University

MO D 5261 and MO D 5110.
Quotations from the Mass Observation Archive reproduced with the permission of the MOA Trustees, University of Sussex.

Imperial War Museum, London

Documentary archive: E. J. Roper 79/2/1; sound archive: Arthur Morris 17840.
Every effort has been made to trace copyright holders and the Imperial War Museum would be grateful for any information which might help to trace those whose identities or addresses are not currently known.

Wolfson Crime, Punishment and Law Archive, Nottingham

Albert Pierrepoint's execution diaries.

Madame Tussauds Archive

Correspondence with Albert Pierrepoint, 1978.

Cambridge Union Debating Society

Record of Debates, 6 February 1978.

Interviews

Tommy Mann, Liverpool and Southport, 2004 and 2005.
Andrew Mitchell, London, 2005.
Fred Wright, Manchester, 2005.
Michael and Doreen Forman, Bromsgrove, 2006.

Film and Television

The Death Penalty, transmitted 24 October 1961.
Tonight: Capital Punishment, transmitted 12 June 1978.
The Story of Ruth Ellis, transmitted 28th June 1977.
Ruth Ellis – A Life for a Life, transmitted 28th November 1999.
Yield to the Night, dir. J. Lee Thompson, GB, 1956.
The Blue Lamp, dir. Basil Dearden, GB, 1949.
Lady Godiva Rides Again, dir. Frank Launder, GB, 1951.